LIFE IS NOW

CLAIM YOUR JOY AND LIVE IT!

Lucie Marlo, PhD

LIFE IS NOW

Copyrights Reserved 2020 © – **Dr. Lucie Marlo**

Disclaimer

The information contained in the book **LIFE IS NOW,** and its related guides is deemed to serve as a part of the author's collection of books, which may increase their revenue and income passively.

The tips, strategies, tricks, and information in this book **LIFE IS NOW** make no guarantee that someone else's research will also produce results synonymous to it. The material can include content or information from the third party, but the author takes full charge of quoting genuine resources that may be subjected to copyright issues. The author takes no charge of the opinion that any of the third-party or unrelated individuals have. If the content inculcated in the publication becomes obsolete due to technical reasons or whatsoever, the author or the publication house are entitled to no blame.

All of the events indicated in the book are the result of primary research, secondary research, and the personal experience of the person(s) involved in formulating the book and bringing it into the form it is in today.

All the content used in this book **LIFE IS NOW** belongs solely to the author. No part of this shall be reproduced, sold, or transmitted in any medium by the third party except after the author's approval.

Contents

Disclaimer ii
Dedications 1
Foreword 2
Introduction 5
Chapter 1: Perspective 6
    Learning How to Control Our Thoughts 8

Chapter 2: Silent Heroes 11
    My Mom, My Hero 11

    Cherish Every Moment 14

    You Are Bigger Than Your Circumstances 16

Chapter 3: Life Is NOW! 20
Chapter 4: Make It a Great Day 23
Chapter 5: Joy Is a Commitment 26
    The Unlikely Picnic 27

Chapter 6: Smile—It's Infectious 30
    Lucas' Smile 31

    A Smile Can Be More Powerful Than Words 35

Chapter 7: Healing Hugs 36
Chapter 8: You Reap What You Sow 41
Chapter 9: Change Starts with You 46
    The Painting *Quest* 49

    If It Matters, Do It Now 50

The Magical Blueberry Patch—Ron's Story 52

Cole 62

Chapter 10: You Will Always Find What You Are Looking For 67

Different Path 68

Chapter 11: Forgiveness Is the Greatest Gift You Will Give Yourself 73

Anger Can Blur Our Vision 73

Chapter 12: When Reality Surpasses the Dream 77

Hopeful Romantic 81

Chapter 13: It's All Perspective…Okay, Mostly 85

A Closer Look at Perception 87

Cut Your Losses Short and Let Your Winners Run 88

Chapter 14: You Are Only Too Old if You Buy into It 92

The Proud Lawyer 92

Defying the Norm 94

Magnifique Papa 95

Chapter 15: Creating Christmas 99

An Old-fashioned Christmas 102

Chapter 16: If You Want It, Bring It 105

Soup for Two 108

Chapter 17: Keeping the Inner Child Alive 111

Play It Again 115

Chapter 18: Kindness Like Confetti 119

    Paper Flowers 122

    Becoming a Healer—Russell's Story 128

Parting words 131

Dedications

I dedicate this book to my beloved mom, Ana, who has been an exemplary figure of doing what is right and not what is easy. Also, to the love of my life, Victor, for being the person I dreamt of being with, and my brother, Sergei, for being an amazing and trusted friend. I adore you and our coffees.

Thank you, Mom, Victor, and Sergei, for your love and continuous support. It means more than you will ever know…

Foreword

Are you like me? I'm a little burned out on books that preach "at" me about how to live a great stress-free, more productive, or joyful life. The authors are excellent at describing the nirvana-like end state but often seriously lacking on how to get there. This book is refreshingly different. It is filled with real-life examples that can serve as an inspiration to living your best life NOW...in spite of whatever is going on right now. It does not describe how to avoid obstacles on the road because truth be told, they are unavoidable. Instead, it highlights and celebrates those who role model what to do when you hit a bump. The stories are enriching and empowering life stories of people who have chosen to claim their joy and not squander it by reliving the past or holding out for the perfect moment in the future.

In Life Is Now: Claim Your Joy and Live It, Lucie Marlo pulls nuggets from her life and experience that others might call rocks or obstacles and artfully builds them into a compelling read. As with any good storyteller, she achieves this without preaching and teaching. She lets the story inspire and guide the reader. She lets the truth of the story encourage us to reach for that elusive "present moment" called life. Although it is clear that the people and circumstances in the book have shaped her, she doesn't lead with her personal epiphanies. She simply tells each story as a witness and allows the reader to take from it what fits their experience and what they need right now. Whether you choose to read the stories in order or you prefer to wander through, "cherry-picking" chapters to personalize the sequence, I'm sure this will be a book you will read and reread. The stories swing open the gate of self-discovery and introspection. With each story, you may find yourself asking: "If this were my situation, could I handle it as well?" or "I wonder if I could do that?"

Ten years ago, when I met Lucie, simply put...I was impressed. She was already an accomplished artist. Her paintings were in established galleries, private and corporate collections across Canada, the US, and Europe. Beyond her creative genius, there was something else. I found her spirit to be loving and resilient even though she had faced down serious health issues that may have left others hard and brittle. She was generous and empathetic in a way that can only be learned by personally enduring hardship. She had immigrated to the West, the daughter of a single mom, with no money or English-speaking skills, but thrived. Lucie approached life with unassuming ease that belied her intellect and credentials. She has a Ph.D. in health and nutrition with twelve years of experience in a clinical setting. She has published numerous articles in health and science journals.

After reading *Life Is Now: Claim Your Joy and Live It*, I now understand some of the amazing people and circumstances that shaped her. The book dives into her world. It is a world filled with an amazingly eclectic range of real people whom she calls friends or acquaintances who, in their unique way, have extraordinary responses to the "cards they've been dealt." Some stories are heartwarming, some heartbreaking, while others are hilarious. She brings these stories to *Life Is Now*. Each story is true. Each story is inspiring and empowering. Each story is a precious gem lovingly offered to you. All of them can be life-enhancing…if you let them.

Without question, Lucie is a gifted storyteller, and she brings her gift to this book. I know you will enjoy it.

Madeline Eason

Introduction

During the twelve years that I worked at a health clinic, I had the privilege of listening to many incredible life stories from patients, people of all ages and walks of life, stories I found not only inspiring but life-changing.

A couple of years ago, I faced a serious health scare. I had long planned to share these stories in a book in hopes of inspiring others. This book was my project for "someday," but this experience was my wakeup call to make my someday projects *now*. Not to fear life, but instead, focus on what is really important, and live life to the fullest.

With the permission of these wonderful individuals, I am grateful for the opportunity to share their stories. It was also fun to include my favorite ones that I picked up along the road of life. This book intends to remind people to smile more and cherish every moment of our precious time on earth.

My wish for you is all the joy, happiness, and fulfillment that comes with gratitude, being in the present, and living an authentic life. I hope that you don't have to go through something traumatic to embrace the gift of being fully alive.

Chapter 1: Perspective

This book has been formulating in my heart and mind for the last twenty years. As human beings, we tend to delay happiness and make it conditional on circumstances that are often elusive.

Examples of this can be found in daily life. I will be happy when I get the perfect job, boyfriend, a certain bodyweight, or a degree. You get the idea. The sad thing about this method is that life is a gift; precious days are going by, days that we can never get back, and unfortunately, a lot of those days don't feel like life is a gift at all.

I started working in a clinic at a very young age, handling the front desk in order to help my mother, not knowing that it would lead to twelve years of work and an education culminating in a Ph.D. in nutrition.

The incredible gift I received was the exposure to real-life stories from people of all ages with various experiences.

Our youngest patient was four months old, and our oldest was ninety-six. The wisdom in some of their stories acts as a guideline for me to this day.

Watching people deal with serious challenges made it difficult for me to be a melodramatic teenager. This experience helped me to become one of the happiest people I know by not taking my health for granted, among other things. It was incredible to witness how some patients with serious diagnoses had an optimistic approach to life, while others with minor injuries seemed crushed by their experience.

In my twelve years at the clinic, I saw everything from suffering to happiness. And for all those years, I looked forward to going to work each day. I did not realize how rare that was, until years later.

Time and time again, I noticed that some people, despite the challenges, managed to find beauty in their everyday lives. They found happiness in the littlest of things. On the other hand, others who seemed to have many gifts bestowed upon them seemed frustrated and dissatisfied. I came to realize that until we learn to appreciate even the smallest blessings in our lives, we will not be happy for long when the bigger ones come our way.

Joy is an inside job. If you find happiness elusive, closely examining your thoughts and perspective, might be helpful. Being aware of our default reactions or thinking about things that don't help us find contentment is important. Most of us never question if the way we think or react to certain situations might be greatly responsible for the reality of our experience.

If you start observing the people in your life who seem to be happy, most of the time, you will notice that they make it easier for themselves to succeed. It all starts by noticing all the blessings that we tend to take for granted.

Life is fluid and forever in motion, always changing, never still. If we wait for the perfect circumstances to be happy, we might end up waiting for a long time. It is incredible how a few simple distinctions can help us discover the power to find joy in adversity and beauty in the mundane.

I hope this book may show you the difference between a life that you love and one filled with pain and frustration.

Life is not complicated. It is we who tend to complicate it.

Learning How to Control Our Thoughts

It took me a while to grasp that we can, in fact, control what we think about, although it is not as easy as it sounds.

I remember when my mother tried to introduce this concept to me when I was going through a particularly challenging time in my late teens. In general, I saw myself as a happy Individual. She implied that, in part, I was responsible for how I was feeling. This frustrated me that I had anything to do with my current unhappiness; it seemed absurd. After all, I was the victim, and it was all so easy to blame the person who had wronged me. Little did I realize that every time that happened, I put myself in the most powerless position a person could be in.

My mother provided me with an amazing gift, saying, "We cannot control everything that happens." We can, however, decide to focus on empowerment, happiness, and supportive thoughts. I tried my best to explain to her how I couldn't ignore the pain I was in. How could I not think about something I found myself stuck in the middle of? She went on with her explanation, bearing the patience of a saint, mentioning that as with television, we could decide to change the channel of our thoughts on purpose. In the most difficult of times, we can try to imagine something wonderful, perhaps a pleasant memory, or think about creating brighter possibilities for the future. This began to make more sense.

Looking back at the challenges of my life, I realized how much needless suffering could stem from our negative perceptions of different situations.

More often, it is actually the meaning we attach to what happens that holds the key to how we will perceive the situation at hand.

> *"Like success, failure comes in many things to many people. With a Positive Mental Attitude, failure is a learning experience, a rung on the ladder, a plateau at which to get your thoughts in order, and prepare to try again."*
> —W. Clement Stone

All too often, we spend precious moments of our life wishing they were somehow different. We waste valuable time that we will never get back by complaining, usually to people who do not have the power to help us change the situation. As humans, we may tend to overanalyze our situations. We entertain negative speculations. We fear and live in future moments. By doing this, we fail to live in the moment, and at the same time, we remain fearful of the future. With all due respect to real-life stress-inducing circumstances such as a car accident, loved ones in danger, or any sort of emergency, most of our daily stress is a direct result of our own thought process. You cannot always control what happens, but you can control how you choose to respond to it.

Remember, it is much easier to change how we think rather than try and change the ways of the world. This may appear to be overly simplistic, but the quality of our life experiences is closely related to the quality of the questions we ask ourselves.

Ask yourself what you find positive about a particular situation, including ones that present a challenge. If you cannot formulate anything initially, continue to ask yourself the same question. You may be pleasantly surprised by the answers that will start to flow. We all have challenging areas in our lives. It is incredible to observe those whom we have known for a good amount of time, as individuals go through a different version of the same problem, time after time again.

In order to dismantle this, we have to realize that as humans, we tend to connect each separate disappointment to gargantuan proportions, leaving ourselves powerless. Along with every new disappointment, we regurgitate all the pain of our past experiences. It is necessary for us to separate our experiences and allow each of them to be assessed individually. By categorizing them into separate scenarios, they no longer seem like an insurmountable mountain.

As time goes by, the words "life is what you make it" sound more and more accurate, because only you possess the power to shape and change your life. For better or worse, the decision lies in your hands.

Chapter 2: Silent Heroes

With one more birthday around the corner, I established a routine of taking a few minutes each day in order to reflect on life. This time, I thought about the people who, in my experience, stood out as examples of strength and courage. These humble heroes have changed my life by providing me the privilege to share their path. I am honored to share their stories with you.

My Mom, My Hero

Me and my mom

When I was around sixteen, I began volunteering at a health clinic. At the time, my mother, who was a physiotherapist and a massage therapist, worked alongside a chiropractor at her clinic. Being a single mom, she worked long hours and was grateful for the opportunity. Long after Dr. Tracy was done for the day, my mother worked evenings and weekends to help her manage other jobs. She could not afford a front desk clerk, and I was happy to carry out the task. She worked hard, and I loved to spend time with her. We would take the bus to work. In retrospect, when I think of waiting for the bus in those vicious prairie winters in Canada, we were happy to be together. We dreamt of a bright future. I guess it was our love for one another and life itself, which filled our hearts and kept us warm.

I still revisit those instances with a smile.

Nearly two years ago, I almost lost my mother when she ended up in the emergency ward for heart surgery. Those months were terrifying for everyone who loved her. We were delighted when she received a clean bill of health a few months later.

My mother, who is one of the kindest souls I've had the privilege to know, became an orphan at age eleven. Her mother died from breast cancer at the age of thirty-one. Her father died in the war when she was just an infant. Blessed with a close relationship with my mother, I could never imagine losing both my parents at such an early age. Despite the various challenges she faced throughout the course of her life, including her health, my mother stayed happy and optimistic and exhibited courage. She is an inspiration for those who knew her.

After years of effort, my mother opened the first of four multi-disciplinary clinics, with me beside her.

On numerous occasions, strangers would walk up to me, often telling me what a wonderful lady she is and about her kind deeds, shaking my hand for simply being her daughter. These individuals would further share with me the wonderful ways in which my mother had touched their lives unselfishly. We worked side by side for many years at our clinic. Working with her was an incredible example of both dedication and compassion for me. She loves people, and helping them was her passion.

She began her career in Canada as a non-English-speaking single parent with four kids. She taught me to face life head-on, to never give up, and to do what is right, not what is easy. At the age of sixty, she completed her doctorate, which had been her lifelong dream. She has been an international speaker and was also given the honor to teach different health modalities in Japan. She volunteered in various women's charities, aiming for the betterment of women facing abuse and teen pregnancies.

> "Have the courage to say no. Have the courage to face the truth. Do the right thing because it is right. These are the magic keys to living your life with integrity."
>
> —W. Clement Stone

I could really just go on and on about this amazing woman, but what I really wish to say is: Thank you, Mom, for being an inspiration.

It is people like you that make this world a better place.

With all my heart, I love and honor you. You have taught me to live with an open heart and not to judge others.

Cherish Every Moment

Despite the present challenges in the world, if we are willing to open our eyes, peace is always just around the corner.

As I sit with a cup of tea and reflect on people and their life stories, Willie always comes to my mind as one of the most inspirational people I have ever had the privilege to meet. Although the world lost him when he was quite young, he had the magical ability to touch the lives of those who were lucky enough to know him.

A beautiful blond, blue-eyed boy, Willie was only twelve years of age and suffering from leukemia when we met. Being a teenager myself, I was not prepared to deal with this situation, and I still feel the same to this day. When I saw this little boy, I immediately felt love and compassion for him. His condition just seemed so unfair. I did my best to be friendly with him and treat him the same way I would any other patient. I was not a good actress; he was able to tell that my heart went out to him. Incredibly, he tried to comfort me. Although this was many years ago, I will never forget what he told me.

He asked me not to feel sorry for him since he had already outlived the doctors' initial prognosis by two years. Willie perceived this time as a great gift. He felt blessed to have spent more time with his beloved family. He said that he had more time to listen to the songs of the birds and enjoy all the beautiful little details of the world around him. But most important to him was that he got to spend more time with his mom.

I remember realizing at that moment that Willie was more spirited than most of us could ever hope to be. In his short lifespan, he managed to find beauty in every moment. He not only noticed but also truly appreciated the things that most of us take for granted. He was grateful and always lived in the present.

I prayed for a miracle to happen. Unfortunately, after four months of him regularly coming to our clinic, I got the news of his passing, I tried hard to remain stoic. I managed to keep it up for almost two days before I burst into tears, sobbing. I knew he would understand that after all, I was simply human and that I would truly miss him. When I think of him all these years later, I find comfort in believing that he learned some of the greatest lessons of life in a short time and that he had moved on to a much better place.

Live every moment…for life is truly a gift.

He will always live in my heart as a champion who was brave and beautiful. Willie cherished every moment of his short life. He had a magical way of letting those around him know about how important they were. Against something so challenging with so much physical pain, he remained strong, happy, and grateful for even the smallest of blessings. Although many years had passed, it was still tough for me to contact his parents, Margaret and Bill. I was scared to bring back any painful memories. They had suffered enough.

I told his story to many people, and it had a profound effect. I felt that it was important to share Willie's story with as many people as I could. This desire helped me to gather the courage I needed to make that call after almost thirty years. I had the pleasure of talking to Bill, who was gracious. Indeed, he was deeply moved by the fact that Willie's story still had the power to change people's lives for the better.

Bill told me about the countless letters that came in from other children, classmates, and Willie's own friends addressing his parents after his passing. They all had shared their unique memories with him; they wished to share their love and appreciation for Willie with his family during the difficult times. Bill told me that when he came to know about Willie's story of helping others to find joy, it became the only way they could make sense of all that had happened. He found great comfort in knowing that Willie continues to live in the hearts of many.

You Are Bigger Than Your Circumstances

When people like Madeline and Jesse end up as your next-door neighbors, you literally need to look up and say, "THANK YOU!" They proved to be fantastic neighbors, and after a while, we were proud to call them our friends. Once, I remember visiting Madeline, who was sitting in her library. We started chatting, and before you knew it, we were talking about her life story. She mentioned that many years ago, her ex-husband left her to raise their three small children alone.

LIFE IS NOW

When Madeline became a single mom, her boys—Bin, Amir, and Mikaal—were seven, five, and two years old, respectively. Times were harsh for them. Even paying for necessities such as water, electricity, and food had become difficult. Madeline told me an endearing story about her two older sons, who were just two years apart, sharing three pairs of jeans for school. By doing this, they always had something different to wear, avoiding any embarrassment. Still, they were a proud family. Madeline emotionally told me about the feelings of her eldest son, who used to share all of his possessions with his brothers. He said that as a child, he actually felt closer to his brothers because of this; they bonded through adversity. This remarkable woman, after many trials and tribulations, managed to work her way up to become one of the top executives at a car manufacturing company. She was financially strong enough to put all her boys through college. Madeline was valued in the company she worked for and, as a result, had the opportunity to travel and lead teams all around the world.

I was speechless, amazed at how she had shared this story with such humility. I realized that I was standing in front of a true figure of inspiration, a hero. Seven years later, I told her how inspiring I found her story and that I wished to include it in my book. Needless to say, I was delighted when she agreed. I was so moved by what she told me that since then, I wanted to use her story as an example of strength and humility. The intent was the same; to share her story with as many women as possible, to remind us that true potential lies within each of us.

If you are stuck in the storm of pain, please remember that life is fluid, shapeless. It is forever changing and that this storm will pass too. My sister said a few times, jokingly, "Yeah, like a kidney stone." Of course, sometimes it is tough, but know that it will still pass. When I asked Madeline about her source of courage to reach that position in life, she told me something fascinating. She said, "I was too afraid to stop, so I kept going." A sad look came over her face as she continued. "Do you know what can happen to African American boys living under those circumstances?" It was clear from her answer that failing was not an option for her. The love she had for her boys gave her wings. They were her strength. I asked her, "What was one of the most important lessons you learned along the way?"

She replied, smiling, "Strong women always think we need to do it all alone, but it was the love and support of other women that made a difference in every step I took along the way."

Many years later, she still refers to a dear friend Annie as an angel. This special lady would make sure her children regularly ate when Madeline couldn't cover food costs. Madeline also talked fondly about a mentor who not only took her under her wing but also cheered for her every step along the way.

She wanted to succeed, and she did.

Her boys are happy, fine men.

She is now married to a wonderful man who knows how lucky he is and adores her. She is enjoying her well-deserved retirement and traveling with the love of her life.

Madeline has also inspired me to start on my next book, *Ordinary Extraordinary People Living Extraordinary Lives.* In this book, I will examine stories like these in more detail, where people do what is seemingly impossible and bring about hope and strength in the hearts of many.

> *"You have powers you never dreamed of. You can do things you never thought you could do. There are no limitations in what you can do except the limitations of your own mind."*
> —Darwin P. Kingsley

Chapter 3: Life Is NOW!

When I was a little girl growing up in an immigrant family from Montenegro, my mother's biggest wish was for us to have our own home. My mother barely spoke English and worked multiple jobs; one of them was being employed as a night nurse. As a single parent of four children, she singlehandedly managed to fulfill her dream with a lot of hard work and the willpower to achieve. I can still recall standing in front of our new home. It was white and two stories. To me, it was the most beautiful place in the whole wide world. My mother looked so happy and proud. I remember her trying so hard not to cry out of joy.

I will never forget the lovely elderly couple who were our next-door neighbors. They were very welcoming and offered us coffee and warm cookies on the day we moved in. After working hard all day, the cookies tasted better than anything else in the world.

This gesture of kindness found a place in my heart. As a kid with an accent, it was nice to be welcomed with open arms. I cannot forget that feeling of pure happiness. I promised myself at that exact moment that when I grew up, I would also be the neighbor who brings cookies and welcomes individuals with an open heart.

A number of years ago, my husband and I purchased a winter home in Scottsdale, Arizona. The recession had hit the U.S around that time, and our lovely neighbors with an adorable little girl were losing their home as a result. We liked them very much; a friendly and hardworking family caught up in the whirlwind of an adverse circumstance. I was so sad to watch them leave from their home. They did not surrender and found strength in the love they had for each other. They told us while pointing to each other, "This is just materialistic stuff; we have everything that matters right here."

New neighbors moved in shortly after them. Although we were unhappy about the circumstances, we decided to give them an old-fashioned welcome into the neighborhood. Thirty years later, I was still excited as a child would be to knock on the neighbor's door, with cookies. I had no idea at the time that the people who had just moved in would become such good friends of ours. Jesse and Madeline are incredible people. Both are active and look at least ten years younger ten their age, a reflection of their youthful spirit. They are kind and intelligent and possess the hearts of gold. I am so happy that they found each other. Every once in a while, you hear something that you instantly know is life-changing, and it becomes a golden nugget for you. This, for me, was one of those moments.

Whenever I shared concern about my future or regret about the past with Jesse, he would look at me right in the eyes and say with great emphasis and confidence: Life is NOW.

He would listen to my worries carefully. Still, he would always remind me that the only thing we have now is the present.

LIFE IS NOW

We learn from the past, plan for the future, but in reality, all we have control over is the present. When we accept this is when life starts getting better.

I was influenced by this so immensely that I decided to rename this book. I would like to thank Jesse. My wish is to share his wisdom with as many people as possible, hoping that it will help others as much as it helped me.

To be aware of the present means to enjoy the tantalizing sensation brought by the taste of each bite of my food, feeling the sunshine on my face and the wind in my hair. I love listening to birds as well as the sound of a thunderstorm.

My husband and I have committed to reminding each other that if one of us inevitably gets off track, we will ask each other what time it is. The answer will be **now**. Where am I? The answer will be **here**.

Cherish all the moments in life. When I catch myself thinking about something hurtful from the past or potential concerns of the future, I remind myself of the wise words of Jesse: "Life is now." Then I get back to the only thing that we really have, the **NOW.**

I'm also happy to report that our old neighbors are happy, healthy, and living in a beautiful new home.

I love happy endings.

Chapter 4: Make It a Great Day

As a young adult working at the front desk of our clinic, I knew a patient who would always say something that intrigued me. Unlike other patients, who would politely say, "Have a great day," he would always say, "Make it a great day."

I noticed the difference, and I liked it. Where one seemed like a kind wish, the other implied that we had the power within us to influence our own day.

Could the concept of "a nice day" be more than a coincidence? It was an intriguing thought that I started toying with. Once, Robert brought his wife to her appointment and waited for an hour for her. I seized the opportunity to ask him more about this. I looked at it as a chance to get to know him better.

Robert seemed happy to elaborate. He told me with confidence that humans are sadly too quick to give in to the pressure of a particular circumstance, whereas exceptional people create their own circumstances. Robert explained that we could choose to look at any situation and find the good in it. The brain, if it stays the course, will find it.

He also believed that in life, you need to decide what you want and then just go after it with confidence instead of the mere hope of it happening someday.

Robert insisted that if you commit to something, you must do everything you can to get closer to your dream, and the next thing you know, you will bring it into existence. I still remember him quoting Walter Anderson:

"Believe in something big. Your life is worth a noble motive."

Robert was an older gentleman who always dressed well and spoke with certainty. He further said that if you commit to having a great day on a daily basis, then it is inevitable for you to live an incredible life. You will train the brain not only to look for the positives but also to look for the opportunities presented, no matter how dark the circumstance.

I still live by his other favorite quote:

> *"When you have exhausted all possibilities, remember this: you haven't."*
> —Thomas Edison

When I think back about some of the most successful people I have ever met, I've noticed that they all have one thing in common: *they never stop learning.*

Any person who performs at the highest level in their field will tell you the same thing; they take every opportunity to expand their knowledge, improve their skills, and build on their expertise.

Robert was no exception. In fact, he told me that every morning he would read something inspirational to start his day, causing him to focus on the positives deliberately. He strictly believed that we needed to train our minds on a regular basis to look for the gifts present in our lives instead of the challenges. "As humans, we tend to spend too much time thinking about our problems with not enough energy left for the solutions," Robert said. "If we focused twenty percent of our time on our problems and eighty percent was focused on a solution, we would fare a lot better in the long run. Unfortunately, without putting in a conscious effort, we tend to do the opposite. As a result, we can be left battle-weary."

In retrospect, this was a man who carved the life that he desired on a daily basis. He had a beautiful marriage, had a great relationship with his kids, and had created a very comfortable living situation for himself. To this day, his incredible attitude is still with me in challenging times. I will always remember him with gratitude and a smile. I am thankful for the privilege of spending some time with him and that he was willing to share his acquired wisdom with me. Robert opened my eyes to the fact that we hold power to make each one of our days the very best it can be.

Chapter 5: Joy Is a Commitment

Throughout my teenage years and early twenties, the fact that I could choose joy seemed ludicrous. Like many, when good things were happening in my life, I was happy. When I was facing difficulties or adverse situations, I felt sad or frustrated.

Like most valuable lessons, life has to offer, learning this one was a long process and would take time and patience. If we don't learn how to handle our emotions effectively, we might feel controlled by our circumstances and automatic responses. Like a leaf in the wind, we are left feeling vulnerable to our surroundings. Eventually, I realized that if staying healthy is a priority, it is imperative to understand how to handle your emotional state. Simply being around positive individuals can help us feel empowered.

When we spend time with negative individuals, it becomes a challenge to stay true to our decision to focus on the positive; we are as good as the people we surround ourselves with. In reality, it is impossible to eliminate negative people from our lives completely. You can only decrease the time spent with them, which will reduce their influence on your life.

A study at the Mayo Clinic confirmed the impact of positive thinking on the quality and length of an individual's life. Researchers interviewed eight hundred Minnesota residents and tracked them for thirty-five years to assess their levels of optimism. Regardless of age or sex, the optimists lived longer. The pessimists, on the other hand, were found to be more likely to die prematurely.

You must have heard the saying, "laughter is the best medicine."

It turns out that there is truth to that statement.

Laughter boosts your immune system by releasing T-cells, which suppress stress-inducing chemicals. Laughter can also boost your energy, making your heart healthier. Sharing joy, having fun, and laughing can result in feeling more connected with those around you, as well as help prolong your lifespan.

Other studies confirmed that happier individuals in the control group did not only live longer but also enjoyed a healthier life. A cheerful attitude is of vital importance to your physical health. It has been scientifically proven that stress has adverse effects on our hormones. Purging one's mind of negative thoughts is essential to overall physical and mental well-being.

Meditation, yoga, breathing exercises, and a positive environment are all beneficial means of minimizing stress and negativity present in our lives.

The Unlikely Picnic

I remembered something over coffee the other day that I want to share with you. A couple of years ago, one of my friends was going through a particularly challenging time. I was determined to find a way to make her smile. I suggested a picnic at one of our favorite places by the sea. She loved the idea. It was wonderful to see her face light up for the first time in months. I packed the goodies, checked the weather, and planned a perfect summer evening after work. We decided to rendezvous at my house.

Sometimes, with the mountains nearby, the weather has a mind of its own.

The next thing we knew, the sky turned gray, and it started to rain. The sad part was that my friend's smile disappeared. "Look, it's just a few drops—we can still go…" Before I finished my sentence, it started pouring.

I had to think fast. I have a belief that always helps me in a positive way. I said to myself, "There is always a way to make things happen. But how?"

She went to the bathroom, and the idea came. I had to work fast.

As she came out, she saw the blanket with all the goodies lying on the floor of my living room. I poured wine into the glasses. I grabbed the flowers from my table and placed them close to the red and blue blanket, pretending this was our favorite park.

She could not stop smiling and laughing.

She joined me on the floor, and we had one of the most delightful evenings ever. Somehow with good food and pleasant company, the hours just flew by us.

We both have many picnics in our life, but we will always remember the one in my living room, with a big smile.

If you commit to happiness, you can stack the odds in your favor of finding it even where it is elusive.

Some simple things we did daily to help her get through this time are a few good examples of what I have implemented into a supportive routine. You can try them out for yourself.

Take a few minutes each morning to notice everything you have to appreciate in your life. Then write them down. This simple exercise strengthens your focus.

Even if times are hard, just try to look for things to be grateful for, and you will find them for sure. By noticing the gifts that most people would take for granted, you will always find something that can make you smile. If you have food to eat, clothes to wear, and a roof over your head, then you are better off than most people in this world.

Developing the habit of looking for things to appreciate whenever our mind has drifted toward problems or challenges may prove valuable to the amount of joy we experience on a daily basis. This is not only a powerful practice but an empowering habit we need to possess. Please do not forget to appreciate your own positive qualities and accomplishments.

Always remember, your mind will find the answer to whatever questions you ask. As I mentioned before, the quality of your life, to a great extent, is related to the quality of the questions you ask yourself. Asking questions such as "Why do these negative things always happen to me?" is a guaranteed recipe for failure. The most important part is realizing that we have the ability to choose what we focus on.

Chapter 6: Smile—It's Infectious

While working on some nutrition-related papers, it became evident to me that our emotions affect our physiology by producing a chemical response. Smiling activates the release of neuropeptides, the molecules that allow the neurons to communicate. They facilitate the brain by indication of the entire body to the extent of our happiness, sadness, anger, depression, and excitement.

The feel-good neurotransmitters dopamine, endorphins, and serotonin are all released when you smile, which not only relaxes your body but can also lower your heart rate and blood pressure. This response goes a long way in helping us to manage stress and even extend our lifespan. The endorphins also act as a natural pain reliever.

Finally, the serotonin released as a result of your smile works like an antidepressant. Many of today's pharmaceutical antidepressants influence the levels of serotonin in our brains.

Realizing that there was a physical response to our emotional state became a turning point in my life. I began to consciously and deliberately look for what is right in my life instead of what is wrong. In reality, both are parallel in their existence. When my day starts off on the wrong foot, I read something uplifting or try to just focus on something that will make me smile. This is a helpful practice that I have developed over time. When I got into the habit of smiling, I had no idea how rewarding it would become.

My automatic response is to smile at children because I adore them. They are so genuine, always living in the present. My mother used to say that an infant's smile is the closest glimpse to heaven on earth.

I also smile at the elderly, and all those people whom I believe could use one. I do it unconditionally, so even if people do not reciprocate, it's okay because I never expected anything in return.

It never ceases to amaze me how often beautiful smiles are returned. I love to look straight into the person's eyes, so he/she knows I mean it. It is not something that I do just for the sake of doing it. Try it out on your own, and the next thing you might notice is that somehow, it brightens your day.

Lucas' Smile

I would like to mention a friend of mine, Mary, an energetic redhead.

I would meet her occasionally at the park I visited whenever I needed some fresh air. I loved to watch children play whenever I'd have a little writer's block. Seeing children happy inspires me. Mary would bring her son every week. She was a delightful person, and I was always happy when we would run into each other.

At one point, I noticed that she seemed distressed much of the time. One day she came to me smiling ear to ear, wishing me a good day. I asked her about the reason for her wonderful mood. The life lesson she gave me was worth sharing. Allow me to narrate her experience.

Joe, her husband, a tall, thin man with a receding hairline, usually came home from work with worry lines on his forehead. When he'd come home, he would hand his laptop to Mary without saying a word. Mary got the impression that it had been another tough day for him. She would often lay awake worried about him.

This had sadly become a routine for her. For the last couple of months, Joe would come home late from work tired and frustrated most of the time. She tried to console him without much success.

Joe's work was demanding. He never intended to bring stress home. However, things were getting out of hand, and he felt unable to control the situation.

One night Joe walked into his son's room when Lucas was sleeping. He walked toward him to give him a kiss on his forehead and sit beside him. Now that Joe arrived late on a daily basis, he missed the opportunity to spend time with his beautiful boy. Weekends were when he usually spoke to him. His son was six years old and in first grade. Moving his fingers through his son's red hair, Joe remembered the moment his son was born. For Mary and Joe, Lucas was the greatest blessing sent their way from God. He remembered the promises he made to Mary about supporting her in raising their only child. But now he found himself as an uninvolved father.

Joe was an ambitious person. His work ethic was excellent. He wished to reach a position where he could build not only security but a great standard of life for his family. Joe also wanted to be the role model and loving father who would always be present for his son, whether he needed him for help with his homework or to learn how to ride his bicycle. He wanted to be there for Lucas.

Joe was watching his son's cute little face, thinking what a beautiful miracle God had blessed him and Mary with. Admiring his son's soft cheeks, he brushed them gently, and his son woke up. The smile on Lucas' face overwhelmed Joe with emotion. Joe tightly hugged his little boy. He held Luca's face and asked him about his day. Lucas' warm hug made Joe feel alive again.

Lucas began with stories of his classmates and concluded with a story of the chocolates that he had shared with the neighbor's daughter. While Lucas was telling him everything, Joe was noticing the joy on his son's face while talking to his father.

After an hour or so, Lucas was fast asleep. Joe left the room quietly to change. Mary brought him a warm cup of tea. He asked Mary to sit with him. Mary was so pleased to see Joe looking happy for the first time in months. The worry lines seemed to have disappeared from his face.

Mary shared with me the conversation that she and Joe had that evening:

"Do you remember when Lucas was born?" Joe asked Mary smiling.

Mary replied with a smile, "How could I forget? When I first held him in my arms, that moment was priceless. It really felt like a miracle." Mary started to laugh. "You almost fainted."

"Ha-ha, yes. I didn't know it took so much for a mother to bring a child into this world…." He took her hands in his and kissed them. "Do you remember Lucas taking his first steps?"

She answered with a grin. "How he ran into your arms…. Do you remember when he spoke his first word?"

"Yes…. It was 'mama.' You have no idea how jealous that still makes me."

"Hahaha." Mary burst into sweet laughter.

Joe continued, "You know why I recall all those moments? It's because today, when Lucas hugged me, I felt all my frustration and worries melt away. As usual, he started with the funny stories of his school, but today, listening to them was different. I found the missing essence of my life and soul today."

Mary asked, "And that is?"

Joe looked in her eyes and said, "It's Lucas' smile, dear. I miss it all too much. When I was with him today, I realized that seeing him every day after work was my primary motivation to finish the job to perfection and then coming home, seeing him smile with excitement because his dad has arrived…. Mary, I am so lucky to have you and Lucas. Your smile, and his, I long for all day. In my desire to give you and Lucas a great life, I realize that I have been giving you and Lucas the rest of me and not the best of me."

Value your loved ones; they are the very essence of life. They can be our motivation and strength to get us through a tough day. Cherish every smile of those whom you love deeply. Make time for them and make them smile as well.

A Smile Can Be More Powerful Than Words

When traveling to a foreign country where we don't speak the language, it is incredible how powerful a smile can be to connect with others, not having to say a word.

While visiting Greece with my mom, at one point in the middle of the street, I just spontaneously hugged and kissed her as I usually do. I noticed that an old man dressed in traditional clothing was warmly beaming at both of us. He seemed to be touched by our display of affection. While smiling ear to ear, he walked toward us and handed a fig to each of us. He proceeded by taking my mom's hand first and then mine. He held them together with his own. At this moment, we all were smiling; there was no need for language to communicate. His beautiful gesture said so much more than words ever could.

> *"Let us always meet each other with a smile, for the smile is the beginning of love."*
> —Mother Teresa

Chapter 7: Healing Hugs

The other day I was pondering the power of the human touch and how valuable it can be. Every human sense has its own gifts. We are able to show love, encouragement, comfort, and passion through touch.

Whenever you come back home after a long, hard day, a hug from your loved ones goes a long way in helping to relieve stress.

Schools in Japan carry out the practice of hugging, shaking hands, or patting students on the back as a sign of encouragement and love at the end of the day. Such a gesture makes students happy when they leave for their homes.

Studies have pointed out the power of physical interaction. A case study was carried out in 1944 in the US that consisted of forty infants. Twenty newborn infants were housed in a separate facility where they had caregivers who would go in to feed them, bathe them, and change their diapers. The caregivers had been instructed not to look at or touch the babies more than what was necessary. The study revealed that infants actually started to die when they were isolated from the human touch. About half of the twenty babies had perished when the study was halted. Before the death of the child, there would be a time when they stopped making any sound, lacking any engagement with their caretakers. They would generally stop moving, crying, with little to no expression. They would then die shortly after that. This was shocking because all types of other care were provided, so this kind of a devastating outcome was not anticipated.

This tragic study shows, in a staggering way, the vital importance of human touch.

We have all seen a child who is crying because he fell and hurt himself. As soon as he runs into his mother's or father's arms, he is pacified and, ultimately, stops crying. That's the power of a hug, which can numb the pain the child felt because of the injury. I understood on a new level the importance of hugs when I met a certain somebody many years ago. He made me realize that hugs have the power to heal internal pain.

I was visiting a patient at the hospital in Winnipeg, Canada, and one of the janitors seemed irritated. He started shouting at everybody walking on the floor that he had just mopped. Nobody really seemed to care about what he was doing, nor his frustration. Everybody carried on with their duties. One of the senior duty doctors came in and warned him about his attitude, which angered him even more. Now, he started yelling at the doctor. "You can take my name up to the administrators! I've had enough of this!"

Everybody was astonished. Nobody could understand his reaction. Then a gentleman intervened. He arrived with his grandfather for his physiotherapy. He was a tall young man. He went to the janitor and hugged him, thanking him for the services he rendered to the hospital. He gave him credit for keeping the hospital clean, grateful to his aid in providing a hygienic environment for the patients to heal.

To my surprise, the janitor hugged him back. He thanked him warmly. His mood changed. There was a bright smile on his face. He apologized to everybody he screamed at and got back to work. I would never have thought that the situation I witnessed could have been taken care of so easily. It is amazing what a little love and appreciation can do.

Out of curiosity, I decided to approach the young man and asked him how he knew what that janitor needed. He said that whenever he visited this facility, he had never seen the janitor disgruntled. In fact, he always seems to be in a good mood. But today was different. He thought that he must be having a bad day and that something unpleasant had triggered his reaction. If the janitor is having a hard time, a hug can at least make him feel appreciated and show him that somebody does care. It will help reduce his stress.

I was moved. I asked him the reason he had behind his belief in the power of a hug. The story he proceeded to tell me was something that will remain with me for the rest of my life.

"Our family used to live in the US. When I was younger, I used to visit my grandfather with my mom. When I reached my grandfather's house, he ran outside the door to hug me. I saw an old man standing at the window of the neighboring house. The man looked at us with gloomy eyes and then went inside.

"I ignored him at that time. Later on, I asked my grandpa about him. He told me that the old man lived alone. His only son had died during the course of the war on terror, serving in the Forces. Since then, he had been alone.

"The next day, I decided to go see him. As it was my first time visiting him, I bought some baked goods. So I went to his house and knocked on the door, but nobody answered. I thought maybe he did not want to meet me, so I went back to my grandfather's home.

"Now, two days passed, and nobody had seen him standing by the window recently. I was afraid that something was wrong. I went back to his house and knocked. There was still no answer. I gently pushed the door open and went inside, shouting, 'Is anybody here?' I could not see anybody, but there was light coming out of one of the rooms. I went inside.

"I saw him lying on the bed. He opened his eyes but didn't say a word. I went close to him and sat by his side. I placed my hand on his forehead and asked him how he was feeling. Tears started to run down his cheeks. He said that nobody had asked him for years about how he was. I wiped his tears and asked him, 'How come you didn't open the door?'

"He said that he thought it was an illusion, a mere figment of his imagination that somebody had come to visit him. He didn't feel like getting up to check just to be disappointed. I was sad to learn that he had spent two days like this in bed. I felt his pain. I helped him get up and then hugged him tightly. He cried for a while, after which I started to see a smile on his face. He began to tell me about his son. Suddenly I saw a young man in his eyes. He was all set to carry out his day.

"He got up from his bed and even made me a cup of coffee. He took me outside to the lawn and talked about soccer, which he loved to play. I was astonished to see that just a hug energized him so much. It was like he had come back to life. His face was glowing. That was the day I realized: hugs can heal. A simple human interaction goes a long way in helping to win someone over, and in this case, to help them feel empowered and cared for."

He smiled at the end of the story and asked me to give hugs to whomever I believe could use one, especially to the elderly.

Be generous with hugs; we never know how much someone might need one.

> *"...we all have the power to give away love, to love other people. And if we do so, we change the kind of person we are, and we change the kind of world we live in."*
> —Harold Kusner

Chapter 8: You Reap What You Sow

Let me tell you a story. Once there was a man named Charles. He was financially settled. Career-wise he was able to accomplish whatever he set his mind to. His achievements were how he liked to define himself.

But something was missing. He often felt sad. Now that he possessed things that he once believed would make him happy, he still hadn't achieved the deep sense of fulfillment, he had hoped for growing up. Charles owned a stunning home, but it felt empty. He dined at the best restaurants, sometimes with his business partners or too often alone. He realized that he craved someone to share it all with, a partner, and a companion.

In reality, he was just lonely.

He decided to meet with those of his friends whom he'd been neglecting for the past few years. He missed them and used to reminisce about the old times. However, whenever they had called him to catch up on things, he would find himself busy. Busy in the pursuit of an empire.

Charles went back to see them, but it did not take him long to realize that he had been taking their friendship for granted. He mistakenly thought that he would still be important to them as he once was.

But reality begged to differ. His friends had gone on with their own lives and learned to live without him. Not out of desire, but out of necessity. No matter how many times in the past they would reach out to Charles, they were always turned down, although politely. Now that Charles wanted to rekindle their relationship on each visit, Charles saw most of them happy. Some were with their spouses, while others were playing with their children. Some were enjoying tea with their parents. Most of them didn't have the best houses, cars, or high-end jobs, but they seemed fulfilled. Their faces were glowing. Although Charles was always welcomed warmly as an old friend, it seemed like he had no place in their life, not anymore. He was deeply upset. He craved the warmth of loved ones, and now in their company, he undeniably felt the void in his own life.

Reluctantly, Charles decided to visit his ex-girlfriend. It had been a long time since they had last spoken. When he arrived, Lisa was watching a movie with her husband. She was surprised to see him but welcomed him warmly and offered him a cup of tea. After a while, Charles asked Lisa if he could speak to her alone. He proceeded to tell her that he had been revisiting the people from his past who had an impact on his life.

"Why do you think everyone I know is in a state of some sort of happiness, except me? I worked so hard my entire life. I made money, built my career, and achieved everything I wanted in life, yet I feel drained and unhappy. I mean, look at the rest of the people I know, including you. You seem happy, and it looks like you are living a fulfilled life. I don't know why that just isn't happening for me."

Charles looked down, afraid of what she would say. He knew that he could always count on Lisa's honesty.

She said, "Do you remember why we broke up?"

He replied, "I...I'm not sure. I really thought things were going well between us. Honestly, being with you made me happy, and things seemed perfect. And then one day you just said our relationship wasn't working out and left. You left me in the cold. To this day, I can't understand why. I thought I had given you the world. But what does it matter now? Why are you asking? You do seem happy being married. I hope you know that I always wished you well."

She replied, "Just before I ended our relationship, I tried calling you. I was crying, I was broken, and I needed you...but you didn't pick up my call. This was not the only time.... You were always busy with something important...something apparently more important than me, which was the point. I thought I'd rather spend my life with a person who provides me with happiness, commitment, time, and makes me a priority."

He replied, "So...wasn't I enough for you? Did I not keep you happy? All those moments, those kisses, those gifts...they meant nothing?"

Lisa said, "Those moments, although beautiful, cannot mean enough if a person isn't committed to their relationship. You have to give love and consistency to be able to get it as well. You have accomplished your goals, built your career, and bought yourself a house, a car, and honestly, everything monetary you had always desired. You never valued the essence of quality time with people who mattered. Sadly, I was one of those people."

He was looking deep into her eyes but had nothing to say. He knew that she was right. So many times, he wanted to interrupt her and tell her that he had been doing enough. Still, he couldn't. He couldn't interrupt her or correct her because she was telling the truth. As an adult, Charles didn't remember spending much time with his parents or siblings. He didn't remember taking Lisa out on many dates, and they were usually on his terms. He didn't even remember their relationship anniversary.

Embarrassed, he left shortly after.

The only things that will flourish in your life are the ones in which you invested your time and energy consistently. Relationships are no exception.

A successful life is a balanced one. All priorities need to co-exist harmoniously. Trading one for the other never works for long.

If you desire love, be loving, give love. If you want happiness, learn to give people a reason to smile. If you expect loyalty, demonstrate it first. If you wish to be respected, learn to give respect first. Treat others the way you would like to be treated in return. Take responsibility for all your actions.

Expecting the other person to know what you need without letting them know will never work in the long term. Clear communication is necessary for a healthy relationship. Make an effort and give your best. Leave no loose ends, and you will soon see others reciprocating.

Even if they don't, you will know in your heart that you gave it all you had. You will have no regrets. Make time for those who matter to you. They are your treasures. Invest your time and energy in them.

Become a mirror that reflects every ray of light falling on its shiny surface. It is always about your decision. You can choose anything, and that includes honesty, respect, time, love, patience, loyalty, or commitment. Once you've made mistakes and learned some lessons, you can become the beacon of possibility by teaching others by example.

There are no shortcuts; this is how it seems to work. Be the best version of yourself, then stand back and be amazed at how things will beautifully unfold around you for the better.

Chapter 9: Change Starts with You

What are the goals that you desire most? What will you regret not doing in your life? What are the things that would keep you smiling every time you think back, knowing you have accomplished them?

Although there are many devastating things going on in the world at all times, something so magical can happen that we take even the smallest steps toward helping others.

I have painfully realized that when I direct a lot of my energy toward the problems in my life, then I don't have enough of it left to deliver the quality of results I am committed to. Instead of allowing yourself to become exhausted by all the injustices, try to become a part of the solution even in a small way.

I am known to be a little of an idealist. When people ask me, "Where do we start? There is so much need in the world," my answer is always simple: **Anywhere!** Who am I to tell anyone what is most important to them? Just look into your heart, and it will tell you.

Whether your primary concern is the health of the planet, our fellow humans, animals, or peace in warring countries, you have the power to make a change.

We all have different gifts and talents that make us unique. Some people can play beautiful music, while others can make fantastic food, or have a burning desire to help.

I believe that if we are willing to bring our different talents together and speak as one voice, then we can be heard loud and clear.

Regardless of the size of the challenge, if we are willing to work with others, we grow stronger. We all have something worthwhile to give. We are not helpless.

This was the concept that inspired me to put together a fundraiser for the Canadian Cancer Association. The idea for this fundraising event had been in my mind and heart for a long time; I was waiting for the "ideal moment" to execute it, and that usually takes a while.

While recovering from the surgery and still waiting for the pathology report, I had more time to think without interruptions than I typically do.

I asked myself, "What are the things that I would regret if I didn't do them in this lifetime?" A fundraiser for Canadian cancer research had been on my bucket list for a long while.

I vowed that I would start to work on it immediately if everything turned out the way we hoped. I was fortunate that life gave me a second chance.

I don't know about you, but I had not found the perfect time to do anything of consequence. Better or worse, yes, "perfect," not yet. In fact, I was waiting for the ideal time to have children of my own, and now I am past the age of when that would be the best idea. Ten more years, and it would be a medical miracle.

Last September, on the day of the fundraiser, I was recovering from surgery. Those were the longest six days of our lives, and we found out that the suspected large tumor was actually a benign one.

I am healthy because of modern medicine; I wanted the same opportunity for everyone. After this experience, I decided to make my someday projects now.

Not to fear life, but to look at what is most important and live it fully. A year later, I was standing on stage, looking around at my family, friends, and community who had come together to help this worthwhile cause.

In the hospital room, this fundraiser was just a dream. Different artists for the same purpose was conceptually born. After a full year of hard work, the moment finally arrived. It took a while to choose the participants. They were all accomplished artists who, like me, made their living by following their passion—a pretty fortunate bunch.

I am a visual artist. I was joined by a First Nation artist, a world-class violinist, a pianist, a photographer, a florist, and a European jeweler—just to name a few.

Our talented chef was, at one point in his life, homeless. After putting himself through school and following his passion, he is finally living his dreams.

This wonderful man possesses a reputation for giving away as many meals as he sells. With the privilege of working with him, I was not surprised when the chef had started gaining attention from the media due to his talent.

Each artist created a unique piece of art from their heart with the intent to raise money for this noble cause. Every artist had their own story, which persuaded them to make their contributions. Together with love and passion, we became one powerful voice.

A dream come true, a fundraiser for the Canadian Cancer Foundation. I could finally cross it off my bucket list.

The Painting *Quest*

I created this painting to send to someone I knew in the world-class cancer clinic. I painted it around the clock, even falling asleep beside it a couple of times. It was devastating when she succumbed to her illness before I had the chance to raise enough funds.

This painting needed to fulfill a promise and to be used for help.

The word *Quest* represents the tireless efforts of many doctors, scientists, and volunteers in the fight against this devastating illness.

A painting that speaks.

The warm colors indicate a bright future. I offered it to be auctioned off with all the proceeds submitted to cancer research. It was tremendous! I felt that finally, it fulfilled its purpose, and I knew my friend would have loved it.

If It Matters, Do It Now

If I was having coffee with you, then the first thing I would tell you is that, if it matters, do it **now**. You may ask, where do I start? That could be anywhere. Listen to your heart, my friend; it will tell you the answer.

You will most likely live a long life, but having accomplished the things closest to your heart, the quality of your life will soar.

You can simply begin by making a list of the goals you'd like to accomplish in your life. Be as specific as possible. You can include details such as what you are planning to do, at what age, with whom you would want to do it, and anything else that may seem important to you.

Make sure also to write down how you would feel if you accomplished your goals and why they are important for you.

Keep that list in a place where your eyes can constantly catch it. Place it on a deck or a piece of paper that you could hang on the wall or beside your computer. By treating the list as a priority and reviewing it regularly, you'll be more likely to turn these dreams into reality.

Every time you achieve one of your goals, check it off the list and celebrate what you've managed to accomplish in your life.

My first husband was an ambitious doctor. He was brilliant at his profession, and his standards were high.

I noticed that he would be really hard on himself when something went wrong, but no matter how much he accomplished, he would not acknowledge his many victories.

I looked at him and said one day, "When do you get time to celebrate your achievements?"

Celebrate your victories. As humans, we tend to beat ourselves up easily. If success is not acknowledged, a person will not feel the ultimate level of joy that they can experience in their lives.

> *"The more you praise and celebrate your life,
> the more there is in life to celebrate."*
> —Oprah Winfrey

The Magical Blueberry Patch—Ron's Story

For seven months of the year, I live with my husband in Victoria, British Columbia, Canada. It is a beautiful and serene place. Old-grown forests, ocean views, and mountains are all an integral part of this charming city. For someone who loves hiking and the great outdoors, this truly is a paradise.

Victoria has some of the friendliest weather all over Canada. We are really fortunate to have a lot of seasonal fruits that are grown locally.

The tasty fruits of summer are always anticipated, starting with blueberries. My husband and I love to go to pick organic blueberries. It is a tranquil activity that makes us feel like kids again.

A few years ago, we found a new place close to our home to collect these marvelous fruits. When we drove onto the property, we noticed that it embodied a sophisticated country style of living. The property belonged to Ron Neil, a well-known and respected local realtor. The blueberry patch was in a sheltered valley bordered by ponds, creek, and old-growth forest.

Like many farm stands in Victoria, this is on an honor system. You pick the berries, weigh them, and leave the appropriate amount of money according to the instructions posted on the gate.

My husband holds a branch of organic blueberries to demonstrate their size. They are even more delicious than they look.

Call me old-fashioned, but I love living in a place where people still work on trust. Once, when we were at the property, we ran into a lovely, friendly lady and talked to her for a few minutes. She was Ron's brother's sister-in-law. Ron was providing a temp safe shelter for her since she was coming from an abusive relationship.

She happily shared the story about the blueberry patch with us.

A number of years ago, Ron's sister lost her son due to a congenital disability in his heart. Ron was devastated by the loss of his nephew. He was also deeply touched by the love and compassion, not to mention excellent care, given at the Children's Hospital in Vancouver.

After joining RE/MAX, who had a strong alliance with the hospital, Ron heard and witnessed story after story of children and families getting exceptional care during their most difficult times.

He passionately wanted to help. In fact, helping the hospital became a driving force in his life.

All the proceeds from this blueberry growth are donated to the children's hospital. Many people who are aware of this enjoy leaving a generous contribution.

As my background is in nutrition, I thought to myself, "Helping kids with an organic farm while feeding people healthy superfood is fantastic. I love this idea."

It was an exceptional example of our own unique ability to find ways to contribute. Ron indeed found a powerful way to give consistently year after year without fail.

Something magical would happen every time we would spend our evening picking berries in this welcoming place. There was a tranquil joy in our hearts, knowing that it served a higher purpose.

The blueberry patch is located in an old-grown forest. With the warm summer wind caressing our faces, we both felt refreshed. Regardless of how stressful our day might have been at work, we would leave with a deep sense of relaxation that would touch our soul.

While working on this book, my desire to meet the man behind this idea grew. After exchanging a couple of emails, Ron graciously agreed to meet me for coffee.

Although a tall man in stature, it only took minutes to see the gentle kindness in his eyes and speech. When we sat down for coffee, I had no idea that my beloved blueberry patch was also one of the many ways through which Ron was giving back to his community and beyond.

I was eager to hear his story.

Ron's earliest memories of "the joy of giving," as he put it, started from being encouraged to "do good deeds" as a scout. He volunteered as one from the age of eight to the time he was fifteen years old. Later on, he started enjoying success in the car business and volunteered with the Kinsmen Club of Victoria and the Special Olympics.

Initially, Ron's connection to the Children's Hospital began as a volunteer assisting fundraising for an annual golf tournament for British Columbia's Children's Hospital in 1998. In the same year, he hosted the first annual Easter Egg Hunt benefitting the British Columbia's Children's Hospital. Ron, who loves kids, started out by buying lots of wonderful Easter treats and hiding them in a nearby forest.

Needless to say, the little ones love it! It started small. "Presently, we have held twenty-two in total now, growing from a handful of participants to a turnout of over a thousand people each year," Ron shared as he beamed a warm smile. It really touched me to find out that some of the first kids who participated, now grown up, love to volunteer, and together they create excitement and fun for the little ones. They recall fondly how much they used to look forward to it and want to give back.

That connection grew further, as Ron volunteered for several years with the Victoria Community for Kids, a fundraising group that participated in raising funds for BCCHF and awareness. They later gained official status and became a part of BCCHF. Once the CFK became an official extension of the foundation with staff and a Victoria office, Ron continued to serve on the board of governors for more than 10 years and continues now on the real estate advisory task force.

In 2004, Ron opened his RE/MAX Brokerage. It has a policy of donating proceeds from every sale that an agent makes to BCCHF. Ron and his team, with their own internal Community Support Fund, collectively look for needs in our community in order to provide them with support. These have included families needing emergency support following house fires, as well as the financial support of families not able to work due to dealing with sick kids. The Brokerage Community Support Fund also funded the Vic West Community Playground.

Ron bought his farm in 2005 and dedicated sales of both blueberries and Christmas trees each year to BCCHF. Ron divided the proceeds of the Christmas tree sales among other organizations, including Mustard Seed, Extreme Outreach, and more.

Every year at the RE/MAX conferences, RE/MAX has an auction supporting children's hospitals. Ron has actively participated by donating a lot of personal objects over the years. Furthermore, Ron's support has also been from bidding and buying items, usually for far above market value. In recent years, Ron has been donating the items back to the Miracle Children who have experienced life-threatening illnesses. It started with a diamond necklace that, after becoming the successful bidder, Ron spontaneously walked over to the twelve-year-old girl and placed it on her. There wasn't a dry eye in the room. Sadly, she passed away about three years later from cancer.

For many years, they raised funds for the former Queen Alexandra Hospital with their Bear Wear event, and they continued to sponsor a tree in the Festival of Trees supporting BCCHF.

Ron and his team supported the annual Ocean FM Radiothon for kids, and I took pies in the face for The Mustard Seed to feed our community's hungry. He not only sponsors but personally, along with his staff, serves hundreds of meals to the homeless three or more times annually, including their Christmas in July. They also donate one hundred turkeys to Mustard Seed at Christmas.

About ten years ago, Ron and his two sons grew their hair. They then shaved their heads for Kids with Cancer on stage. Unlike most men our age, Ron actually has a full head of beautiful hair. All joking aside, he became an excellent example for his kids to see the power they had to make a difference at such a young age.

On that note, perhaps my favorite of Ron's stories is when he decided to help in building an orphanage in Mitanni, Uganda. They also funded and helped build a school for the orphanage.

This is Ron, happy to see these kids happy.

He told me: "I have been fortunate in my life." Ron did not want to be a man who simply wrote a check. Instead, he packed up with his sons Cameron and Justin, who were fifteen and twelve at the time. Ron not only sponsored the project, but the three of them were a part of the crew who literally built the orphanage. WOW! As my husband will affirm, I am not often speechless.

I had the pleasure of speaking to Ron's son Justin, who now is twenty-two. I asked how this experience impacted him, and if there was anything he would like to share with others. Justin, without any hesitation, told me that this experience had a profound effect on him. The first thing that really struck him was how little these children had, and yet they seemed so happy.

They were so grateful for any help. Justin remembers how wonderful it felt to contribute to them. He loved knowing that they could make a significant difference for his new friends. Justin shared with me that he asked permission and stayed with the children at the orphanage for two days.

Justin and his dad Ron will always cherish these moments.

For Justin, this was a turning point. He said that he felt privileged as a child and wanted to spend the rest of his life, finding ways to contribute. How powerful to understand at twelve that you have the ability to change lives for the better. His dad being a beacon for his two young sons.

Ron's motto is "Live to give!" And this wonderful man is certainly doing just that. People like Ron remind me of how big and beautiful the human spirit can be. It is incredible how much good a man with a big heart, who is a visionary, can do by inspiring his community to join and help others.

This world is a better place for having him in it.

LIFE IS NOW

Proud supporters of our community, Ron Neal and The Neal Estate Team provide support to the following charities:

AIDS Vancouver Island	Greater Victoria Coalition to End Homelessness Society	Saanich Neighborhood Place
ALS Society	Greater Victoria Family Services	Saanich Volunteer Services Society
Alzheimer's Society	Greater Victoria Housing Society	Silver Threads Service
Ballet Victoria	Greater Victoria Public Library	Spectrum Community School
BC Cancer Foundation	Habitat for Humanity	Spinal Cord Injury BC
BC Children's Hospital Foundation	Headway Victoria Epilepsy and Parkinson's Centre	United Way (60+ member agencies)
BC Schizophrenia Society	Heart and Stroke Foundation	Victoria Cool Aid Society
Beacon Community Services	Hospital Bear Wear	Victoria Dragon Boat Festival
Big Brothers and Big Sisters	Inter-Cultural Association of Greater Victoria	Victoria Hospice
Boys and Girls Club	JDF Midget AAA Hockey	Victoria Hospitals Foundation
Camp Imagine and Auxano	John Howard Society of Victoria	Victoria Immigrant & Refugee Centre Society
Canadian Cancer Foundation	Kings Kids Ministry Orphanage Uganda	Victoria Minor Hockey

Children's Health Foundation of Vancouver Island	Learning Disabilities Association of BC	Victoria Rainbow Kitchen
Citizens Counselling Centre	MS Society	Victoria READ Society
Claremont School	Mustard Seed Food Bank	Victoria Royals
CMN Miracle Home Program	Northridge School	Victoria Sexual Assault Centre
Community Micro Lending	Open Door	Victoria Single Parent Resource Centre
Cridge Centre for the Family	Our Place Society	Victoria Symphony
Discovery School	Pacific Christian School	Victoria Therapeutic Riding Association
Farmlands Trust Society	PEERS Victoria Resources Society	VRCMHA Bantam AAA Hockey
Garth Homer Society	Queen Alexandra	YMCA
Greater Victoria Citizens' Counselling Centre	Saanich Minor Hockey	

It was indeed an honor and a privilege to shake hands with Ron Neil. You will always remain an inspiration. Thank you, Ron.

Cole

A happy family

Lindsay and Brad were married with no kids. They decided that instead of wasting nights and weekends on television and activities that wouldn't fuel their souls, they would instead do something good for the world. They were determined to find a way to serve their community.

Brad was asked to participate in a charity called St. Baldrick. He was deeply moved by the following facts that he learned across the journey:

- More children are lost to cancer in the US than any other disease.
- 1 in 285 children will have cancer in the US before they turn 20.
- Worldwide, cancer is diagnosed every two minutes.

These staggering statistics, as Lindsay put it, shook them off the couch to start brainstorming about how they could contribute to making a difference. Lindsay warmly shares with me that "parents and families that have children diagnosed with such diseases and are fighting for their lives do not have time to fight this disease, so we felt compelled to help them."

After a short while, Brad became one of the top fundraisers of the event.

Lindsay and Brad boldly decided to host their own St. Baldrick's event near their hometown in Illinois, a location that had never experienced a fundraiser like this. The main objective was to raise funds and for family and friends to show support by shaving their hair at the event. This would be a sign of solidarity for all those children who are suffering, showing that we are with them. We support their journey.

Lindsay and Brad ended up hosting this event for five years, raising over $250,000. This effort was mustered with typically six months of planning. We would spend our time and energy finding silent auction items, raffling items, hanging posters, doing radio interviews, advertising in the newspaper, and locating professional hairdressers, DJs, Irish dancers, bagpipers, and more.

Brad put everything he had into this event and sacrificed many hours in order to dedicate his time, effort, and energy to what these events needed. Lindsay looked at him with newfound admiration. All of a sudden, her best friend turned into her hero. Lindsay, at this point, didn't realize that Brad had this sort of dedication and strength toward the suffering.

In the first year, Lindsay and Brad met a family that touched our lives forever. The family had a small boy who was fighting for his life in the hospital, so we decided to "sponsor" him, which included honoring his journey at our event. He wasn't able to fight cancer, but he lived his life to the fullest until the end.

From the sidelines, Lindsay and Brad thought and prayed for this family. The world stopped spinning for that family when they lost their child. Lindsay and Brad weren't directly a part of their journey, but it directly impacted Lindsay and Brad's entire life. It affected the way in which they viewed the world. Lindsay looked down and told me from the heart that:

"All of a sudden, our issues were small and attainable."

Whenever their lives get challenging, they think about this little boy. They think of Cole's strength and his mother's, and remember that life is precious and not to be taken for granted.

"We should value each breath and moment that we all have together," said Lindsay with a warm smile.

During this time, Lindsay and Brad struggled to have a child, often finding themselves looking longingly at couples with children. They had to accept that there was a possibility that it wouldn't work out for them. Almost eight years later, to their great joy, Lindsay and Brad found out that Lindsay was pregnant.

They talked about names and decided that if they had a boy, his name would be Cole. They both wanted to honor the inspirational boy in the hospital who had lived on in their hearts. After all, Cole had changed the way they looked at the world. He gave them hope that people are good and want well for others.

They said, "Since then, we see the world in a positive light that fills our hearts with appreciation and forgiveness."

Lindsay and Brad decided to write to Cole's mom, Dawn, to ask her for her blessing in using her child's name for their son. They wanted Dawn's family to know that the boy gave them such hope and that he still brings joy and goodness into the world on a daily basis. He has not and will never be forgotten.

Brad brought Lindsay to the doors of the hospital at 7 p.m. on a Sunday night, after parking their car. Lindsay was mentally preparing for the procedure that lay ahead. She checked her Facebook account quickly and received a message from Dawn's sister. She was so grateful for the hope that they had instilled in Dawn. She said that she had barely seen her sister smile in years, and now she had a wide smile on her face.

They had a baby the next morning, and that message gave Lindsay a lot of strength and support.

The doctor held the baby up and said, "It's a BOY!" Cole went home with Lindsay and Brad that week.

"I know that he has an angel with him. We are so grateful to have him in our lives," said Lindsay, with tears in her eyes.

They traveled back to Illinois to visit Dawn so that she could meet Cole. She said that he looked just like her baby boy, with blond hair and blue eyes.

"We can only hope that our Cole brings as much joy into this world as her boy did," said Lindsay.

What started out as the heartfelt wish of a young couple to make a difference for others brought priceless gifts into their own lives. They are more in love with life and each other as a result.

We meet a lot of people daily, but we cannot deduce the impact they can bring on our lives. People like Cole, Lindsay, and Brad leave an affirmative impression on our lives that can bring out the good in us. No matter how distant of a memory they become for us, they will never be forgotten.

Chapter 10: You Will Always Find What You Are Looking For

Too often, we tend to look at ourselves through critical eyes. We look for what is wrong, rather than what is right. Remember the most powerful computer in the world: your mind. It will find the answers to whatever you ask.

For example, if you ask yourself, "Why do I always seem to put on weight?" you will most likely get an answer such as you don't have enough willpower to control your appetite, which will not make you feel much better.

On the other hand, if you ask yourself how you can lose weight or keep it off, an answer that will support you in your quest will pop up in your mind automatically. It will think of a proper recourse. Booking an appointment with a dietitian might work. Learning about different exercises that support your health would be helpful. Finding an exercise you actually enjoy will increase the odds of continuing with it over the long term and making it part of a healthy lifestyle.

Becoming aware of the questions we ask ourselves all day long is crucial. By consciously asking better questions, you will increase the odds that the answers will support you toward the path of your desire.

Different Path

As much as I love people, once in a while, someone comes along who likes to challenge the humanitarian in me.

Among other professionals, I worked with two physiotherapists. They were both fantastic and possessed stellar reputations. For this reason, we would often receive some severe cases recommended by different doctors. One time, there was a new patient who had been in a serious car accident and needed much care.

It was difficult to see a young man barely being able to walk into the clinic and obviously in pain. My heart really went out to him. I spontaneously ran to open the front door. He looked up at me with a cold stare. He was tall, heavier set, and clearly looked angry

Living in the Canadian prairies, I always made sure to have warm tea and fresh coffee available all the time, especially during the long winter months. When I offered him something to warm himself up, he did not even bother answering and just looked away. Now I was perplexed. I handed him the questionnaire for new patients with a smile; however, at this point, I was not expecting one back. He didn't disappoint.

Our physiotherapist, who was a lovely person and a friendly man, greeted him with hospitality. After his treatment, the new patient promptly paid and left without a word. Although I knew he needed help, I was not sure if we would ever see him again.

A pleasant woman called later that day, booking several treatments for him. I figured that he must be feeling a bit better and wanted to come back.

Treatment after treatment, things went pretty much the same way. He spoke only when necessary and was usually in a bad mood. He certainly made no effort to hide his general discontentment. One day I had enough of his behavior and referred to him as Mr. Sunshine. He did not seem amused, but then again, I did not have much to lose. I was hoping he would get the memo and put in a bit of effort. Unfortunately, there was no such luck.

It was, however, really rewarding for all of us to see him walking faster and straighter after only a few treatments. It was moments like these that made all of our efforts worthwhile.

One evening he was our last patient. A young lady came in with him. She was beautiful, and unlike him, had a pleasant personality. I wondered, it had to be his wonderful sister who loved him unconditionally; after all, wouldn't she have to?

After he went into the room for his treatment, she remained in the waiting area with me. I offered her a cup of coffee, and she graciously accepted with a smile.

I was confused but happy to spend time with her and hoped she would accompany him in the future.

She looked at me and smiled. Out of the blue, she said, "He wasn't always like this, you know. He really is a wonderful person. We're engaged to be married, and I'm scared that he might change his mind and call off the wedding." Now I was even more confused. I thought to myself, WHAT!!! He might call off the wedding instead of thanking his lucky stars daily? I know love is blind, but this is ridiculous.

If I knew her better, I would have been tempted to tell her to put on her sneakers and run while she still had the chance. But I resisted, and it was a good thing I did. She looked down and quietly said, "Everything changed after the accident." She was trying not to cry.

Rebecca explained that he was everything she'd ever dreamed of until the accident. He was thoughtful and fun, and they could not wait to get married. They thought that life couldn't get much better when he got accepted to the local professional hockey team. The future was bright. He was a brilliant hockey player, and it was his passion. He could not imagine himself doing anything else. In a few moments, everything changed. The accident was ruled the fault of the other driver, but this did not make him feel any better. Day after day, the physical pain this poor man had to endure was nothing compared to the emotional one he was feeling inside. No longer being able to play hockey, which was his passion, devastated him.

He was overweight, and at this point, it was hard to imagine that he had been an athlete. Wow, this all started to make sense. Rebecca was determined not to give up on her beloved. She knew in her heart that the man she had fallen in love with was in so much pain that it became hard to recognize him.

As he came out of the room, my gaze followed him when he looked at Rebecca. She could not see him, but it was clear to me that he was in love. When she noticed him, he quickly changed his disposition to one of a person who was in a bad mood and angry all the time.

Mr. Sunshine's next appointment was late in the day. In fact, we were closing right after him. I was the last person on duty to leave, and we were alone. I decided to try to have a conversation with him. I felt really sad for what had happened to him. I was hoping that he could find joy again before eventually alienating the lovely woman determined to love him.

As he was leaving, I mentioned that I was sorry about what had happened with the hockey team. He turned around slowly, and I could see he was furious. I have to confess that I became nervous. He started shouting, "She told you? She had no right!"

It was the first time I had a patient yell at me; I tried to keep calm. It wasn't easy. I looked right in his eyes and said, "That is enough," with a voice that made it clear that I meant it. He became silent for a while. He just sat down, looking broken, and said, "She had no right to tell anyone."

At this point, I sat down beside him, placed my hand on his arm, and said gently, "Do you want to know what else she told me?" He just looked down but did not move his arm. I took that as a good sign. "She told me that she loves you and she knows that you are still the wonderful man with whom she fell in love with and that she was terrified that you would call off the wedding."

He looked up at me and said, "I was planning on calling it off" and started to cry. With my hand on his shoulder, I asked with concern, "Why would you do that?"

He said, "Rebecca is terrific, but she feels sorry for me. She does not have the heart to leave me like this. I don't want to destroy her life just because mine is."

"She just wants the 'real' you back, the man who was thoughtful and fun. He can still be here, hockey or no hockey," I said.

He listened quietly. "Has there been anything else that you have wanted to do?" I asked him.

He looked at me and said, "One thing, but I am not smart enough to become a chiropractor. I did always find it interesting."

I said, looking at him, "You were smart enough to pick Rebecca."

He smiled. It was a rewarding moment.

Next time he came into the clinic, to the surprise of all working there, he was pleasant. He continued to improve in every way.

Unfortunately, hockey would not be an option at a professional level, but Rebecca and Mr. Sunshine did get married, and the last I heard he was loving chiropractic school.

She was happy to tell me that when school would get difficult, he would remember that healing comes in many forms. He wanted to give people the support that he had been given when he needed it.

Life will always give us a possible path. Just because it is not the one we first envisioned, it does not mean that it will not work out. I believe with all my heart that he became a wonderful healer.

Chapter 11: Forgiveness Is the Greatest Gift You Will Give Yourself

In order to heal completely from any emotional trauma, one needs to forgive.

Unfortunately, sometimes people misinterpret the word *forgive*. To forgive does not mean to agree with some terrible injustice. It only means that you need to stop feeling angry or resentful toward someone for an offense or mistake that has hurt you. Being furious continuously can negatively affect not only your fulfillment but your health too. The sad truth is that it can unintentionally hurt the ones closest to you, as well.

Anger Can Blur Our Vision

When I worked at the front desk, we had a patient coming to us for her physiotherapy due to intense back pain. I used to talk to her while she waited for her appointment. As we got to know each other better, she started to share about different aspects of her life with me.

She was an aspiring woman. Catherine, a blue-eyed brunette, had two daughters who meant the world to her. At that time, one was twelve years old, and the other was ten. As a mother, when she put them to bed every night, she would kiss their foreheads and think about giving them all the love they deserved.

Then she would go to bed as she had to wake up early in the morning in order to reach her clinic. When you are working hard the entire day with different patients, it makes it easier to sleep. You sleep because you are tired and not because you actually want to sleep. For Cathy, it didn't help much. Something kept her awake late at night. Whenever she lay down on the bed and closed her eyes, a glimpse of the past would hit her, and she would get up.

It was her ex-husband. The memory was of a betrayal. She still remembered everything that had happened two years earlier. The memories didn't blur. She had caught her husband red-handed with his secretary in a hotel room. The heartbreaking flashback broke her from within.

Sometimes she picked up her cellphone to check her inbox for messages from him. It usually had two unread messages at the end of each day. He used to text her daily, asking about kids with an apology for the past. Cathy wasn't able to accept it. He had broken her heart and her trust. How could she forgive him for cheating when she was ready to die for him?

Every morning, the girls woke her up with a smile and kissed her cheeks. Both were loving and cheerful, but they also asked her a question to which she had no response. They asked her, "Mom, why doesn't dad come to see us?"

David wanted to see the children, but he was not ready to face Cathy until she forgave him.

She would run to the kitchen, avoiding the question, and ask them to get ready as per the routine. The reality was that no matter how badly she tried to ignore the situation, it came in front of her every day. Her daughters missed their father. She could not replace him.

One day after dropping off the kids at school, she gathered the courage to pick up the phone to call David. Cathy invited him for dinner on the weekend.

She decided to accept his apology. Now David could come home to visit their daughters easily. She chose to stay separated from him, but for the sake of her daughters, she decided to forgive him.

The act of forgiveness made her feel at peace and light. It was important for her daughters, as well. She kept their happiness above everything else in her life.

When David came one Sunday with candy for their daughters on her invitation, Cathy immediately felt her eyes well up with tears, seeing her children so happy to play with their father.

When David left after dinner, he left a note for Cathy. It stated,

> *"You looked beautiful, as usual. Thank you for doing this favor to me. I don't know how I can conclude this, but it was great to see you all happy and together."*

After reading this, tears rolled down her eyes; then, her younger daughter hugged her from behind. Cathy turned toward her and picked her up in her arms.

Her daughter wiped her tears. Cathy was thrilled to see her daughter's face glowing. Now she felt as if the weight of the world had been lifted from her shoulders. The love for her daughters gave her the strength to forgive, which became the source of her relief.

What I gathered from this instance was that we need to forgive others, not because they are necessarily entitled to receive it, but because we deserve inner peace. Always remember, forgiveness is a gift you give to yourself.

> *"The weak can never forgive. Forgiveness is an attribute of the strong."*
> *—Mahatma Gandhi*

Chapter 12: When Reality Surpasses the Dream

We have all gone through days that feel effortless, where everything works out the way we want it to. Traffic seems to part as we drive, and the perfect parking spot opens up just a second before we pull right in.

I believe that one of the keys to joy is being vigilant enough to recognize magical moments while still living them. My husband and I have adopted a supportive habit of saying, "It cannot get better than this" to one another out loud whenever we feel it. While I am writing this excerpt, I am sitting in the backyard of our winter home in Scottsdale, Arizona.

My husband and I are both Canadian citizens who emigrated from Europe. We both love Canada and are no strangers to the extreme winter. It is January 31, and I need a calendar to remind me of this fact.

I am warm, happy, and enchanted by the rugged beauty of the sunny desert. It was not so long ago that this house was a dream, and today I am living in it. I am afraid to pinch myself.

My loving husband kisses me and brings me a cup of coffee. "It cannot get better than this." He just finished the paperwork for my dream car, a Mercedes-Benz SL 550.

For days after my dream car was delivered to our door, I would slowly open the garage door, thinking it was a dream. When I would reopen my eyes, and it was still there, it was hard to believe that it was actually mine.

I paint for a living. I am glad that I never gave up on my passion previously when it seemed like an "unrealistic dream."

I spent a significant part of my life "logicking" (my invented verb) everything to death. Following what my brilliant sister, Marie, told me, "If we ponder over anything for long, we always find a way to logic ourselves out of it," and it made sense.

Logic often brought me security and predictability, but on the other hand, it had a way of sucking the magic out of my life too. Slowly but surely, I decided to pursue happiness, which often conflicted with logic.

When you are happy, your presence becomes a pleasure for your surroundings. When others see you achieving your dreams, it makes them hopeful in the form of motivation for their hearts to help them in pursuing their dreams.

One of the factors that I found to be the toughest to understand was how to get out of my own way while I was dreaming big.

"What if things don't work out my way? What would people I respect, think?"

It would be something like, "I thought you were smarter than this."

I love the French saying:

> *"The one who never risks can never win." These days I am allowing myself to go for it!*

I remember going for bungee jumping in my late twenties. It seemed silly at that time. I lovingly refer to it as an idiotic sport.

While I was going through a painful time in my life, I volunteered to drive a friend to fulfill his dream of bungee jumping. He was afraid of heights and not physically well. He felt the need to take charge of his life. It was a symbolic start for "jolting" himself back into life. I really appreciated his intention and was happy to support him.

I had no intention of jumping myself, just driving. Once we were up there, it became irresistible. There is something magnificent that happens when we look at fear right in the eyes and act anyway. It is so invigorating!

I had no idea how therapeutic it would be. I felt completely alive for the first time in a few years. It might not be the best example that one could use, but you get the idea.

My sister, who had a young son whom I was really close to, was not impressed. She told a friend of mine that she was surprised about me going for this "stupid chance." After all, what would she tell my nephew if something happened?

He replied with a smile. "Auntie adored you and life. She was happy and lived fully." My sister shared this with me. I will never forget it."

That is precisely how I want to be remembered many years from now, hopefully. I make sure that those whom I love know it as a fact. I don't think that you can show people too many times you appreciate them. I will continue to look at my fears straight in the eye and act anyway. I intend to be grateful and live every precious day to the best of my abilities in gratitude and awe.

> *"We can only be said to be alive in those moments when our hearts are conscious of our treasures."*
> —Hornton Wilder

Hopeful Romantic

When I was young, my friends always accused me of being a hopeless romantic. I would jokingly correct them and say, "I am not a hopeless romantic since I remain hopeful about love." Therefore, I am a "hopeful romantic."

I had a great relationship with my family and friends. I loved my career. I lived in a wonderful community in which I was involved. Still, I felt like something was missing. If you would have asked me about the wish that was closest to my heart, then honestly, I would have had to say "that one great love." I never wanted to end up in a mediocre marriage like the many people I knew.

I wanted romance, magic, and lasting passion. I dreamt of love being immense to the extent that long after our time on earth, it would remain in the hearts of those who knew us as an example of what is possible.

I was discouraged by well-meaning family and friends. They would tell me, "What do you want? In time, all romance will dissipate. Magic is present when you're dating rather than when the everyday sets in."

After a couple of failed relationships, I started to question myself. "Did I really ask for too much?" My dream continued to burn in my heart. It was undeniable. I would always say that somewhere out there, and there is a man sharing the same vision. I was determined to find him, regardless of how long it took.

A few years later, I met the love of my life. He was also ridiculed for his idealistic dream. Seventeen years of marriage and counting, and we're still madly in love.

We work at our relationship regularly, ensuring that we make quality time for each other when the obligations of life inevitably get in the way. We both want romance, so we plan special weekends for each other away from our busy world. At times we love to play tourists in our city and spend a night at a romantic location close to home. Sometimes we dress up in formal wear for a special candlelit dinner at home. It is so fun to dazzle and surprise each other.

When people ask me what the secret to our marriage is, I would simply tell them: Keep doing the things that made you fall in love in the first place in order to stay in love.

It always puzzled me how, as humans, we are happy to go to great lengths to impress someone new. As life becomes busy, it becomes easy to get lazy and to start taking the person with whom you decided to share your life for granted. In reality, this is the person to whom you must give your complete effort and attention. Someone trusting you with the rest of their life is a big deal. I see it as almost sacred.

When young couples tell me that they don't have money to go away with each other, I am certainly sympathetic. It took us a while to get there too. The good news is that it requires no money to use your imagination. Candles and spring flowers picked by your loved one can make you feel appreciated and cherished. A warm bath together or simply packing up dinner that you were planning to have at home and taking it to a nearby park will add variety and an element of surprise. Leaving little notes for each other can be fun. Call your imagination into play; it can be rewarding.

In order to keep the magic in our lives, we need to first believe that it is possible.

Talk regularly with one another about your wants. Dream together, and most of all, don't let anyone tell you that it is impossible. Sometimes I think that our marriage is even more magical than what I dreamed could be possible in my youth. My husband proposed to me in Italy. It still remains our favorite place to visit. It was incredible to retrace our steps on our tenth anniversary.

LIFE IS NOW

This picture is from our last trip to Italy, where we revisited our favorite places. This is my love and me in Tuscany visiting a location of sentimental value; it was an absolutely magical moment.

Chapter 13: It's All Perspective...Okay, Mostly

My husband and I were driving back home to Victoria, Canada, from Scottsdale, Arizona.

We had been wintering in Scottsdale for nine glorious years. Sometimes we traveled through California and other times through Utah. Although, in the beginning, we did stop in Napa and a few other lovely places. For the last few years, though, we just could not find the time.

For years, I had heard that Bryce Canyon in Utah was spectacular. I really wished to see it. Victor and I adored nature and were always looking forward to driving through Utah since it is uniquely beautiful.

This was the year where I was not ready to make further excuses, and we were all set to go. We started looking into the distance and accommodations.

I started to feel like an idiot when I realized that our detour would be about thirty minutes longer than the original route we would usually take. After everything was booked and the whole trip was planned, which also included a few business meetings, I caught the flu along the way for the first time in eight years.

I was running a fever when we reached Bryce Canyon. Since the moment of our approach and arrival, I could not believe my eyes. Rock formations, the color of corals, began to emerge in front of our eyes, and evergreens grew from pink coral sands. It all seemed like a fantasy.

We could not guess what was coming up next. The next stop was more beautiful than the previous one. I included a picture since mere words could never do justice to it.

Tourists from all over the world were smiling ear to ear. They, unlike us, had to travel far to get here and were happy to do so.

I could not believe that for a thirty-minute detour, it took us nine years to see this breathtaking place. I have been fortunate and have traveled extensively. I have to admit that this was one of the most magnificent places I had ever seen.

This experience left me wondering as to other times in life when we might perceive the obstacles to be larger than they actually are. How many times was something so magical within reach, and yet we passed it thinking it was much more challenging than it was in reality?

We don't tend to regret going extra miles; we seem to regret the times we didn't even try. One thing I can tell you is that you should not wait for the perfect time; it tends to take a while.

There will be a lot of stops along the road of life. It is said that it is not how many breaths you take but how many moments take your breath away.

Bryce Canyon definitely enchanted both of us, but more importantly, it taught us to find out facts and not make assumptions. It does not always have to be hard to be worthwhile. As the kids would say, "Thirty minutes, really? Not cool."

A Closer Look at Perception

I like to ponder perception. The perception seems to be nothing more than our own slanted view of reality. Based on our past and experiences, we develop ways, supportive or not, of evaluating things.

Try to catch your automatic reactions toward something that would normally challenge you. It helps to realize that there are many ways to look at the same situations. If we look for the blessings even when they are not obvious, we are more likely to find them. The same is the case with problems or analyzing your life. Don't be afraid to look at things from all aspects. Sometimes it helps to write things down on paper. This will stop us for a while at least form overthinking the challenge at hand. This exercise can add a clear and fresh way to see the current circumstances and help put them in perspective. Try to remove yourself emotionally from the challenge and ask yourself what you would advise a dear friend if they were in your shoes.

Speaking of friends, if you are lucky enough to have someone in your life whom you deem much wiser than yourself, then you can seek their help to analyze the situation. If not, then it might be a good idea to start actively seeking out this kind of person. Their presence can be invaluable in your life.

Remember, your perception is the reality of your life experiences.

Cut Your Losses Short and Let Your Winners Run

My husband trades in the markets. He loves it! Although it is stressful, he finds it invigorating. He enjoys challenging his mind.

I wanted to understand his passion so that I would know more about what he loves to talk about. Thus, I went to a three-day course.

I heard something that weekend that I thought would apply well to all aspects of life:

> *"They could not stress it enough: You need to learn to cut your losses short and let your winners run. In other words, when the market is going your way, let it run. Keep a watchful eye. Don't panic or pull out because you have a bit of profit.*

LIFE IS NOW

"On the other hand, when it turns against you, cut short. Do not make it personal trying to prove yourself right in the market or in our case, life."

I thought to myself that if only we learned to apply this regularly to our lives, then many of us would have a different story to tell.

Sometimes we work tirelessly for years toward a goal. The excitement that accomplishing a goal brings seems to fade too soon as compared to the amount of effort we put in. On the other hand, when facing a challenge such as a simple cold, it seems to take the lead in our mind and our speaking.

What if we celebrated or at least acknowledged even the smallest victories? Many of us have stopped noticing our blessings.

I am a Canadian citizen who emigrated from Europe. The standards of life in Canada are among the best in the world. The majority of the world does not enjoy the many things that we here tend to take for granted.

You will be able to find what you are looking for if you are seeking an answer for what is wrong. The powerful computer sitting inside your head will find an answer every time. If you ask it to start noticing the things you are grateful for, then your brain will look for more things to appreciate. The positive and the negative surrounds us at all times. It depends on what you are looking for.

Like most people, if you're putting yourself down, and figuring out all the reasons why you can't change or have what you actually want, your problem isn't a lack of education, sex, age, or the many other stumbling blocks we put in front of ourselves. You've got a perception problem. You're looking at yourself in a disempowering way. If you transformed the way you view yourself, your whole world would begin to change.

Today, I am healthy thanks to God, happily married, and have close relationships with family and friends. I am painting full-time and have my work in corporate with private collections in Canada, the United States, Europe, and South Africa. I have serious art collectors as my clients. The reason I am telling you this is because, believe me, this was not always the case.

All I really did was change my point of view of myself. I started asking myself better questions. I started exploring how to make something possible instead of focusing on why it could not work for me.

One of my favorite quotes comes to mind:

> *"If you think you can or think you can't, either way, you are right."*
> —Henry Ford

Please think about this story for a few moments, and relate it to your own life.

Look for what you want, not what you don't want. Remember that your brain will find the answer. Ask as many times as it takes to find a suitable solution. Improve the quality of your questions, and you will find a way to improve your life.

But don't just look at it in a general or superficial way; go further than you ever have gone before. Look beyond the reasons you've come up with and why you can't change or get what you want until you "see" a way to improve your current circumstances.

Chapter 14: You Are Only Too Old if You Buy into It

These human beings really made me realize that age is just a number. Please share their stories with someone who may need to read them.

The Proud Lawyer

Jennet, a petite blonde, was a patient of my mom. She was a single mother and worked hard to give her kids a good life. While waiting for her appointment one day, she shared a thought-provoking conversation with me that she had had with a younger friend over coffee.

Jennet told him about her regret concerning not being able to finish school. Her dream, when she was younger, was to become a lawyer and help others. In fact, she was already starting her legal education when she found out that she was pregnant.

Jennet had to join the workforce to earn money and hence removed studies from her priority list. Now that she was in her early forties and her kids were more mature, it felt too late. Her friend encouraged her to go back to school, but in her mind, she just couldn't.

"I will be forty-seven by the time I finish," she cried. Her friend wisely told her: "You will be forty-seven anyway. It's up to you as to whether you get there with or without your dream."

LIFE IS NOW

I have to tell you, and this made me think as well. This statement helped Jennet find the courage to go back to school.

Jennet was a humble and calm person, but at times she questioned her decision. It was probably due to the fact that she was struggling. Every night, she thought about whether she had made the right decision or not.

With studies and a job to support herself and her kids, Jennet used to stay up late at night to complete her assignments and work. She would spend any free time she had with her girls.

One night, when she reached home, she rushed to the kitchen to prepare dinner for the kids. She had dinner with them and then went back to her study table to provide a finishing touch to her thesis. The weekends were ultimately busy, as she had to complete chores around the house and go grocery shopping.

We kept in touch during this time. Sometimes it helps to have someone just listen. I could not have been happier when Jennet finally graduated.

I took her for lunch to a top-notch restaurant in our city to celebrate. I was thrilled for her. She looked so beautiful and proud. The sense of accomplishment she felt was visible on her face as well. Jennet told me that she would have never permitted herself to go back to school if it was not for the conservation she had had with her friend. That discussion made all the difference in the world and allowed her to become what she had always dreamed of.

The best part for Jennet was that the girls were so proud of her. They told her that she was an inspiration and thanked her for her courage. They mentioned that it was because of her that they were no longer afraid to pursue their own dreams. It makes me wonder why we, as individuals, limit ourselves from life-changing opportunities because of our age. Possibilities are endless when we place our minds and efforts toward our goals and believe that age is simply a number, whereas success can be achieved at any point in our lives.

> *"It is never too late to be what you might have been."*
> —Mary Ann Evans (*George Eliot*)

Defying the Norm

Tom, a slender older gentleman with a beard, was going through depression after losing his wife to cancer. At that time, he was a patient at our clinic. In order to keep himself distracted, Tom decided to continue his education in philosophy, a lifelong passion. He went back to school and enrolled himself in a Ph.D. program for philosophy. Not everybody has the willpower to turn their adversity into an opportunity.

Although he really struggles at times, day by day, he transformed his struggle into inspiration. Going to school at this age and catching up with the curriculum was challenging, to say the least. In the initial stages, he faced many hurdles, sometimes with students and teachers, along with understanding and memorizing the course material. Despite these factors, he never gave up. Every time he faced a hurdle, he tackled it courageously. He believed in defying the odds and proving himself capable of fulfilling his dreams at his advanced age.

Tom also started fencing during the same period at his university. This was another dream he had abandoned many years earlier.

When he completed his Ph.D., he was seventy-four years old. He received a standing ovation from the university as he was the most senior student to graduate. In his valedictorian speech, he dedicated his degree to his beloved wife. He said that her memories gave him the power to rise again, and if she were still alive, she would be the first person to believe in his capability of pursuing a Ph.D. and that she must be proud of him in heaven.

He also fought valiantly against depression. This was demonstrated by the fact that he no longer required any form of medication. His sheer willpower and positive mindset made this possible.

He made me understand that you just need to believe in yourself. No matter what, if you trust yourself, you seriously increase the odds that things will work out. Just push the accelerator and get going. Perceived barriers such as age cannot prevent a determined individual from succeeding, regardless of limiting notions that our society possesses concerning age.

Magnifique Papa

Raymond, my stepfather, came into our lives when we were adults. Other than my younger brother, the rest of us lived on our own for some time. Raymond, who came across as a kind person, was very easy to like. He was handsome, but most importantly, to me, anyway, was that he truly loved my mother. It was heartwarming to see my mom in love after many years on her own. I guess the charming French accent didn't hurt his chances of winning my mom's heart. Then again, who could blame her?

Although he was several years older than my mom, one could never tell by looking at him. He was of an ideal weight, in great shape for a man of any age. Raymond was a restaurateur and had spent time in some of the loveliest parts of the world, including Chevre D'Or in the village of Eze in the south of France.

Enjoying a visit with my stepdad. I must say that the time spent with my parents is always precious.

LIFE IS NOW

He had also lived in England, Spain, and the United States for some time. In all fairness, I have rarely encountered people in the restaurant business in this kind of shape. Daily temptations do not make it easy to resist the fantastic food and wines that are always accessible. He was a disciplined person who enjoyed everything in moderation. As I got to know him better, I realized that being active is still an integral part of his life.

As the years went by, Raymond became a dear part of all of our lives. He always made us feel welcome in their home.

After some time, Raymond shared with me about his childhood. After losing his mom as a child, he went out on his own to face the world at the mere age of fifteen. He worked hard his entire life until finally retiring in his early seventies. In his heart, he always wished to learn martial arts. He shared his dream with my mom, who encouraged him wholeheartedly.

At the age of sixty-four, he enrolled himself in kung fu lessons, which had been one of his lifelong dreams. He loved it! After much hard work and endless hours of training and practicing at the age of sixty-nine, he received his first black belt.

Raymond diligently continued training, and at the age of seventy-seven, he received his second black belt with a standing ovation from his peers, teachers, and all attendants. He became an example of possibilities to all those who knew his story. We took him for a celebratory dinner to one of his favorite restaurants. People who overheard the story lined up to shake hands with him.

Raymond did not let his age come in the way of fulfilling his dream. He had the courage to follow what his heart desired and, by doing so, opened the door of possibility for all those who heard his story. He is, indeed, an inspiring person. Today, Raymond is eighty-three years young. He still walks five kilometers daily and even goes to the gym three times a week.

He reports no aches and pains and enjoys the quality of life of a much younger person.

As we age, it becomes essential to remain active in our lives. This can be achieved through various fulfilling activities such as volunteer work, hobbies, studies, and other interests. Many people find that these tasks will help them in maintaining optimism in their later years.

Exercising, particularly some strength training, has been proven in recent years to help dramatically with preserving brain/memory health. Mentally challenging activities are imperative in preserving brain functions at an advanced age. Teaching or taking a class, reading, or even doing crossword puzzles have been proven beneficial in keeping the mind healthy and active.

Unlike Raymond, I never liked to exercise, although I do recognize its incredible value. Whenever I don't feel like being active, I remind myself about his astonishing discipline and willpower. He has become a beacon in the lives of many. He is enjoying a full and well-deserved retirement with a big family who adores him.

Chapter 15: Creating Christmas

My husband and I spend our winters in beautiful Scottsdale, Arizona. With a background in nutrition, I always look forward to visiting the Old Town Farmer's Market on Saturdays. Seeing an abundance of fresh vegetables and fruits makes my nutritionist's heart sing.

That market is a feast for all the senses. The aroma of deliciously cooked food and freshly brewed coffee is so tantalizing. I find it heartwarming to hear the sound of people talking, laughing, and simply enjoying this welcoming place with friends and family.

The market features different bins with a variety of greens, all priced the same. Spinach, mixed greens, and arugula are my favorites. In order to fill a few bags with all the healthy goodies, this becomes a process that inevitably lasts a few good minutes.

One Saturday morning, while selecting greens for our weekly salads, I accidentally overheard a story that touched me deeply.

Chris, a man, working at the market who just ran into a friend, was positioned directly behind the salad bins. I was brought up that it was not appropriate to eavesdrop on other people's conversations. However, the circumstances made it virtually impossible to tune out.

At a later date, Chris generously shared the details with me over coffee. At first, I felt really uncomfortable to tell him that I had accidentally overheard his beautiful story. I wanted to ask him if he would let me share it in my book.

This is the story I overheard in parts. I hope it stays in your heart like I know it will remain in mine.

Chris's older brother Mike had a successful liver transplant and was doing well when he was diagnosed with terminal cancer.

Chris had made a point to visit his brother often during his illness. One of his last visits was in December when he thought it could be his brother's last Christmas.

The night before Chris was to leave, he had a hard time sleeping, and he realized that his brother would not be decorating the house for Christmas, something his brother had loved to do. During their childhood, the holidays had often been stressful. However, when Mike moved to Nebraska, he started to enjoy the joy of Christmas and decorated the house both inside and outside every year until he got sick. Chris realized that under the circumstances, the house wasn't going to be decorated. He came up with a wonderful idea: to decorate the outside home in hopes of bringing a bit of Christmas joy to them.

It was 2 a.m., and Chris was working outside despite a temperature of 18 degrees (-7 Celsius). The love for his brother kept him warm. Chris determined to bring the magic of Christmas to his loved ones, decorated the outside of the house, including the tractor, which Mike cherished.

The next morning, Mike and Joyce saw what Chris had done and smiled ear to ear. For a few magical days, Christmas was back. They were, for a short time, able to take in the spirit of the season. Mike was so pleased that he personally set up his Christmas village in the house, bringing the joy back full circle.

Chris and Mike reminisced during his visit about their mother—a strong and kindhearted woman. She was always happy to help anybody who was less fortunate. Although Chris and his brothers had a very modest childhood financially, there was plenty of love and somehow still enough to share with others.

When they would question why she helped so many, even though they had their own struggles, she would simply say, "It takes more energy to walk around a problem than to simply deal with it."

To me, these are words full of wisdom to live by. I have kept them in mind ever since.

In retrospect, I believe that I was meant to hear this story. Christmas can be a stressful time of the year for so many. No matter how challenging the situation becomes, if we are willing to dig deep into our hearts, there is always some love we can find. Some kind of light that we can make emanate from within the deep recesses of our hearts.

Love is the supreme and ultimate power and has the ability to bring magic to those who need it the most, irrespective of circumstances.

Chris and Mike pose in front of their family tractor, which Chris decorated to honor his brother almost fifty years later.

An Old-fashioned Christmas

Some years ago, my family and I decided to do something different for Christmas. Like many other families, we all worked hard. This quality time with loved ones was cherished by all of us.

My older sister had made a suggestion one Christmas when we were busy opening our gifts.

Marie remembered fondly and shared with us some of her favorite Christmas memories from our childhood. Being the eldest, she remembered most clearly the toys our mom used to make for us as kids. As a newly emigrated family, there was no extra money to go around. At the time, I believed in Santa; it took me years to figure out that long after us kids went to sleep, my mom spent many sleepless nights making toys for us.

Marie and the rest of us remembered these particular toys as some of our favorites. Out of her story, the idea formulated. Next Christmas, we decided as a family that instead of buying each other gifts, we would make them. Everyone seemed excited by the concept—a little intimidated, but mostly excited.

We created some fun rules of engagement. Everyone would participate with no exceptions. Working long hours, I had to start early in the year. As soon as February arrived, the all-new Santa's helpers began working.

The following Christmas, there was different magic in the air. It was incredible to witness what love can create. My sister made me handmade and painted pillows. I hand-painted a unique Christmas ornament for every family member. A kitchen stool and side table were a wonderful surprise for my sister Chris. This was a team effort. We were all in awe; it was amazing. As the evening progressed at the dinner table, we all took turns talking about the experience of actually making gifts instead of buying them.

There was a similar thread in all the stories. The time and love that went into making the gifts brought back the true meaning of Christmas to our family. While spending many hours creating each gift, we all found ourselves thinking about the person for whom we were individually making a gift. This made us refocus on how much they meant to our lives. Although our world seems to be getting busier and not slowing down, we did, unfortunately, go back to buying gifts.

It's funny that even after almost twenty years, we all still remember the old-fashioned Christmas as our favorite. I still count the handpainted pillows my sister made me as some of my most cherished treasures.

Chapter 16: If You Want It, Bring It

In May 2019, after a four-decade absence, my sister Chris made the trip to Montenegro, our ancestral homeland, to revisit the places of her childhood and reconnect with relatives. Montenegro is a small country with many natural charms but a turbulent history. While things are improving steadily since the breakup of Yugoslavia, many issues remain, including the lack of animal shelters and the overpopulation of stray dogs and cats.

One big happy family

As the rain clouds cleared in the late afternoon, making way for the Mediterranean sun, Chris strolled down the promenade along the beach. Before long, a beautiful blond dog, similar to a Labrador retriever, joined her. By his playful demeanor, she could tell he was a young dog. He was teasing her, nipping at her backpack, and inviting her to play. She stroked his head, and he soaked up the attention. Chris thought of her own two rescued dogs back home, half a world away, and felt sad for Oscar, as she had already named him in her mind. She could already picture him sitting contently among them, in the warmth and comfort of a loving home. It broke her heart to think of her new friend as living on the street, without the necessities, food, clean water, and shelter.

Chris thought that at least she could get him something to eat from one of the numerous seaside restaurants. Oscar followed her for a while but then disappeared into the crowd that was beginning to gather as dinnertime was approaching. She looked for him into the evening and the next day, hoping he would return to the promenade. Unfortunately, he was nowhere to be found, and she had to leave a couple of days later to return home. Oscar was not the only stray. Many, many dogs and cats were fending for themselves on the streets, and Chris' heart broke a bit for each one. An overwhelming sadness set in as she boarded the plane for the long journey back.

Days and weeks passed, but she could not get Oscar out of her mind or the many other dogs she had encountered on her trip. Despite the distance and the magnitude of the task, her sadness turned into a determination to make a difference. Through an online search, she found an organization helping strays in Montenegro, staffed by volunteers. They offered to look for Oscar. Agonizing days went by.

The volunteers sent her photos of several dogs who matched the description, many beautiful creatures in need, but none were Oscar. Chris could not adopt them all, of course, but she felt compelled to help in some way. She created a fundraiser, selling her own handmade jewelry, with every penny going to SAM (Stray Aid Montenegro), a nonprofit organization dedicated to helping save stray and abandoned dogs and cats.

Eventually, the volunteers located Oscar and learned that he had an owner, who like many, let his dog roam the streets without a collar. Chris was relieved to find out that Oscar was okay, but she still worried about him and the others. It was clear that shelter and education programs were desperately needed. Chris became a member of SAM. Through the organization, she sponsors several dogs in foster care and continues to raise funds for spay and neuter programs, food, and vet bills. She works on facilitating adoptions within Europe and finding ways to make adoptions in North America easier.

While searching for Oscar, Chris came across two dogs in particular and fell in love with them long-distance. She saw a tiny photo of a small, furry face with a black nose and dark eyes. The eyes looked large against the white fur. They were unsettled, fearful eyes. They took her breath away. Those eyes called her across the distance, across the ocean. She knew she had to make the fear in them disappear. She had to save Archie, this little creature, this little white dog so far away. Then there was Belka. Her eyes spoke of intelligence and hardship, of a turbulent life lived, of loss and of survival, of inner strength and courage. In the dog's weary yet resolved eyes, she saw the same hardened stoicism in the faces of the people of the region.

Chris needed to overcome many challenges to bring her new rescues home, including indifferent airlines and outdated regulations. After trying to arrange cargo transport for weeks, Chris flew to Belgrade to meet up with the volunteers, who drove the dogs all the way from Montenegro. Chris flew home with her new charges in tow. Archie and Belka quickly adapted and now enjoy the comfort of a home, a warm bed, toys to play with, and regular, healthy meals.

This story has a happy ending, but we cannot forget the countless other strays. Life on the street is brutal and short. Most puppies do not reach adulthood. Hunger, disease, and motor vehicles are a constant threat. This inspired the creation of SAM (Stray Aid Montenegro). They run spay and neuter programs, help with emergency vet care, find foster homes, and facilitate adoptions. SAM is staffed exclusively by volunteers and funded by donations, and it needs help to save lives. Please consider making a donation and spread the word about SAM and the very important work they do.[1]

Soup for Two

I live in Victoria, British Columbia, Canada, for half the year. It's a breathtakingly beautiful island situated close to Vancouver, British Columbia,

---

Website: www.strayaidmontenegro.be
Facebook: https://www.facebook.com/groups/2127576480842064/
Instagram: https://www.instagram.com/stray_aid_montenegro/

and Seattle, Washington. The population consists mostly of an older demographic who have come to the warmest part of Canada after retirement.

I moved to Victoria within days after turning twenty-nine. It was some time ago, and I became accustomed to meeting the elderly by living there. I figured that on the bright side, it was safe, and wild parties would not tend to be a problem.

My heart did, however, really go out to the many elderlies whom I would meet, especially the ones who had been widowed. I could see much loneliness and sadness in these people who once used to be energetic and productive individuals. I tried to do everything I could for the few widowed ladies who lived in the same condo complex as me, sometimes by going over to vacuum or just by helping them carry their groceries.

I did notice that just taking time out to sit and listen to them seemed to make a lot of difference. Once in a while, I would make a large pot of soup that I was eager to share with one of them.

My mom made homemade soup since I was a kid. It is incredible how often a bowl would end up just in front of the right person. Sometimes it was someone who needed a meal, but most of the time, it wasn't only about need but the love and comfort that was shared through food. This simple gesture can have a powerful effect on people.

Like my mom, I loved sharing soup. I would take the soup bowl and sit down with my neighbor, who had been widowed recently. We would share a bowl, and then I would leave the rest for her. I hoped that not only would they have some healthy homemade food to eat but that the warm conversation would linger a bit with every bowl.

It is hard to describe just how fantastic sharing food and time with people who need it really can be. I hope this simple idea, which is easily duplicable, will spread to different communities. It is incredible how a little effort can go a very long way in providing happiness. In retrospect, the warmth of interaction did seem to linger with me as well.

I read the following as a child, and it had a profound effect:

> *"How lovely to think that no one need wait a moment. We can start now, start slowly, changing the world. How lovely that everyone, great and small, can make a contribution toward introducing justice straightaway. And you can always, always give something, even if it is only kindness!"*
> —Anne Frank

What are the needs in your community? What are the unique talents that you can share with others? Don't ever think you are powerless. Big or small, all acts of kindness make a difference.

Spending some time alone and listening to our hearts can be so rewarding. Please don't accept the word *impossible*. It is not even in my vocabulary anymore. So many things that were once thought impossible surround us right now. People could not even imagine something as colossal as the internet some years ago.

Chapter 17: Keeping the Inner Child Alive

When was the last time you played in the rain? Danced to your favorite music, or watched your favorite cartoon from childhood? We all have a child inside us that is usually lost as we juggle through the many obligations of life. We need to find a way of keeping our inner child alive. Otherwise, we can suffocate a vital part of ourselves.

One of my friends, Blake, didn't give much importance to this advice of mine until he began to feel choked in his "picture perfect" life. He had to experience it in order to realize how necessary it was to his life.

Blond and well-built, Blake was someone who laughed hard while showing me a bald spot on his head, which was actually a hair disaster that his barber had committed. When his younger sister needed someone to test her cosmetics on, he would volunteer with a broad grin on his face.

I have known him for a long time. He was a cheerful person before. He would always seem happy and readily smile at strangers. But that smile seemed to have vanished as he became a little older. His face turned dull day by day. I could see the spark in his eyes fading, and I didn't like it. I missed his old happy and cheerful self.

Blake became the successful head of Marketing for a multinational corporation. He was committed to his work and responsibilities to the extent that most of the time, he could not even make time for himself.

Though he drove an expensive car and lived in a beautiful neighborhood, he was fed up with his routine and felt low-spirited. Every day he used to go to the office and attend meetings to climb up his career ladder. He started to miss the joy he used to have in his life.

Blake used to scroll his cellphone occasionally to view some of his pictures that he had taken on his vacations. He found himself smiling through photos while skydiving and visiting Niagara Falls, etc. However, the images appeared dull to him now despite his bright smile in them. He tried to get some peace of mind by visiting every famous destination in the world for vacating, but he still felt like he was tired, frustrated, and energy-less. He felt like something was missing in his life. There was some kind of void that wasn't being fulfilled. He loved playing the guitar, but now he didn't find joy in that either.

Every evening, tired, he closed his eyes while he lay back on his sofa to try to relax.

One evening, while on the sofa, he suddenly heard the sound of thunder. He got up and went toward the window to check the weather. It had started to rain. Contrary to his younger self, who would have rushed outside to enjoy the rain, he began to think that he should check on his baby girl Kristy, whom he thought was outside.

He could see raindrops falling on cars and trees around. The dew drops began to cover the window. He turned his head toward the backyard and saw his four-year-old daughter with soft pink cheeks and sparkling eyes playing hopscotch in the rain. The same thing that he used to do when he was her age, and even many years later.

Being the protective father he was, he ran outside in order to bring Kristy in. After all, she could catch a cold. As he stepped into the backyard, where his daughter was playing, she ran toward him while dancing in the rain and dragged him with her to play.

Accidently, Blake soaked his feet not only with water but with mud. "Kristy, we need to go inside; otherwise, you'll get drenched and catch a cold."

"But Daddy, I'm already wet! It's so much fun and look, so are you." She was looking at Blake with innocence in her eyes.

"No, honey, come on, we need to go inside…"

Kristy took a few steps away from him and said, "But…but…this is a time to play, Daddy…"

"Catch me." She continued and started to run in the backyard. "If you catch me, we will go inside…okay, Dad?" she shouted from a distance. This was a baby entrepreneur in the making, Blake thought to himself. Only four and closing deals. This witty child.

Blake ran after her to catch her, but he missed her every time. One part of his heart said that he should just pretend to catch her and let her play. After all, this was the time when a child learns to be free-spirited. However, the other part asked him to be a responsible father. He had to take her in. She collected the raindrops in her hand and then threw them on Blake. The water nearly went in his eyes. Still, he had begun to enjoy himself.

After all, she was four. She went out of his arms or dodged him, passing between his legs, and no matter how hard he tried to catch her, Kristy doing her best amazed him. In an attempt to catch her, Blake started to play around. As the rainwater began to gather on the ground, he and Kristy began to jump in it together.

Blake finally began to enjoy the rain. Both of them were soaked. Now, Kristy was sitting on his shoulders and telling him how she was trying to catch the biggest drop of rain for him. He was the best father, Kristy told him. Blake felt every drop moving over his face. As Kristy ran toward the puddles, Blake followed her, and they both jumped over puddles, skipping each of them.

They danced together, ran together, and tried to catch each other. He stretched his arms wide. It was like he was embracing something abstract. It was his inner child. He could smell the soil. His face started to glow in bliss, and he started to smile.

Listening to their giggles, his wife Bonnie came out. Blake ran toward her and took her in his arms. "Put me down...," she said. She didn't expect her mature husband to be playing in the rain.

He brought her in the backyard under the rain. Bonnie insisted on going inside, but Kristy and Blake held her outside in the rain. As per Kristy's idea, the family played Ring a Ring o' Roses in the backyard, under the rain. They let it pour on them. He sang his favorite songs, and Bonnie danced with him, holding the hands of their daughter. Blake wasn't a good singer, but this was how he had asked Bonnie to marry him. This brought back that wonderful memory.

They were happy playing in the rain, like kids. All this reminded Blake about the fun he used to have as a child. He was able to understand what I was trying to communicate by that time about the importance of nurturing our spontaneous carefree child from within.

Maybe, words didn't work; thus, it had to be shown in practice—or felt.

That innocent smile was something one could not get from anything else apart from keeping their inner child alive. It wasn't something complicated that they did, but it was an act of finding joy in the simplest of things, something as simple as dancing in the rain.

Play It Again

Even after many years, I still remember the following life lesson with a smile. I had found out that we had a new patient coming from out of town. He was an established comedian living in Los Angeles at that time.

His profession was a mirror of his personality: cheerful and lively. He liked to visit Canada, so an annual tour was on his list. Whenever he came to our city, he would book a treatment at our clinic due to an old injury during skiing.

My mother and I would always be happy to hear from Tony and looked forward to his visit. After all, not every patient could make us double up with laughter. He was dark-haired with a slightly receding hairline. A character face but handsome in his own way. Tony was intelligent and charming, but most of all, hilarious.

Tony was featured in some of the best television shows in the US at that time. He also won an Emmy Award for his outstanding writing. He was dating a gorgeous model and moved in the circle of many famous celebrities. At the mere age of nineteen, it was a world that I could only read about in magazines. Be that as it may, he was down to earth, and that was something I really appreciated.

We stayed in touch for a long time. We became good friends. Once, he surprised my mother and me with tickets to his show. He had them delivered to our doorstep. This was a rather exciting way to find out about his visit to our town.

Being a headliner, Tony was to be introduced by a young and new comedian. The starter comedian seemed nervous and was fumbling from the start. He noticed that the front row table was filled with around twenty ladies. In hopes of getting a desperately needed laugh, he started bugging them by making jokes like: Where are the men? Modern women don't seem to have use for them, etc. There were a few laughs, but they were downright reluctant. He just couldn't connect with the audience.

He tried to engage a lovely older lady who was not responding. He said, "And how did you get rid of your husband?" as he tried to turn it into something funny. To which she yelled out that he had passed away recently.

She said that the ladies in her life were attempting to make her smile. This is why they brought her to a comedy club. She started to cry and promptly ran out of the room. It went from bad to terrible within seconds.

I could understand by the mortified look on the young comedian's face that he did not mean to hurt anybody; it just all came out terribly wrong.

People felt bad for the widow and started heckling and throwing food at him in disapproval. I still remember him trying to cover his face and clothes while a chicken wing drenched in sauce hit him square in the forehead before my eyes.

The opening comedian walked off the stage, humiliated. I felt sorry for him. It was just an innocent mistake that turned into a blunder. I also felt terrible for my friend, Tony, who was supposed to be announced by this time.

After the welcoming music played, the lights flashed, and the announcer tried to warm up the crowd. Tony was welcomed coldly by the furious audience. Most of them still had their arms crossed and eyes frowning.

Someone viciously heckled him as he walked onto the stage. He gave it right back. This went on for a bit, and the audience now started jeering Tony. His powerful act was off to a terrible start.

A great idea came into Tony's mind. He picked up the microphone and told the crowd: "I promised you a great show, and you're going to get one." He called on the announcer and said, "Bobby, introduce me again." Nothing happened. Bobby, confused, failed to introduce him.

Then Tony yelled, "Play it again, Bobby. Reintroduce me like you mean it."

The audience was quiet and confused. The announcer started playing music, and the lights flashed on. Once again, with "From sunny Los Angeles, the one…" Tony ran out onto the stage with a different energy. He was warm and smiling.

He started telling great jokes, one after another. Before too long, the audience began to reciprocate his level of enthusiasm. The show went on for more than an hour. The room just kept on growing stronger with energy and, of course, laughs.

I have seen many shows, and this was the best comedy show I have ever been to. At the end of his performance, Tony got a well-deserved standing ovation.

I would like to admit that I have used Tony's brilliant idea of reintroducing myself more than once in my life. It worked from everything from a date to a job interview.

Sometimes things take a wrong turn in the start, and circumstances that are out of our control can make situations even more challenging. Whenever things don't turn out in your favor, don't give up too soon. Start again. It's incredible how one can turn around adversity with the help of commitment and imagination. Sometimes all we need to make things better is to start again. We can find a way to reintroduce ourselves as many times as it takes to be the best version of ourselves.

Chapter 18: Kindness Like Confetti

Giving does not precede receiving. It must be understood that the true gift lies in giving for the sake of giving and not with the intention of receiving anything in return. That, I am afraid, I would have to call *trade* and not a true gift.

While working at a hospital, I heard wonderful stories from our patient Clair about a remarkable woman who had touched her life. She used to visit the hospital where Clair worked every Saturday. Whenever this lady came in, she brought a lot of gifts for the patients. The presents included flowers, scarfs, bracelets, keychains, etc. Whenever she knew that any patient had a birthday coming, she came in with balloons. Regardless of their ages, she would find a way of making them excited like a kid. Not to mention, it was also heartwarming to see those suffering patients smile.

She used to visit patients with so much warmth that a person standing in front of her could never feel that she was virtually a stranger. It was always like she was talking to someone in her family.

The first time our patient, who was a nurse, saw her, Clair thought that she might be related to a nineteen-year-old patient suffering from cerebral palsy. She was consoling the patient as he wept, and when she began to leave, the boy kept on asking her to stay. Clair couldn't think of strangers developing such a connection until then. Clair told me that the lady had been visiting the hospital regularly. Clair described her as older with a spark in her eyes and the smile of an angel.

She came only to spend quality time with patients. She'd ask them what they wanted and listened to their stories. She had a beautiful voice and used to sing their favorite songs for them.

Her face was always glowing with happiness, and this was accentuated by the smile she gave the patients, whose day she had surely made a whole lot better. Clair was curious to find out the reason why she visited so often. She didn't even have anyone that she personally knew admitted at the hospital. Clair was amazed. She wanted to learn more about this unusual lady.

Once, while Clair was taking a break and sitting in the reception area of the hospital, she saw this lady entering. She took this to be an opportune moment. Clair went to grab two cups of coffee from the place next door, and when she returned to the hospital, the lady was still there. Clair didn't want to miss this chance to talk to her alone. She asked the lady if she would join her and that the second cup of coffee was for her. She smiled with an affirmation and asked Clair to take a seat.

While they sipped their coffee, they randomly discussed the hospital and the staff. She told Clair that she knew that she worked there and that she had observed her a lot of times working with patients.

Clair told her about her days at the hospital. The ladies were really enjoying sharing stories over coffee. Clair could already feel a connection developing between them. It didn't feel like they were talking for the first time, but in fact, it felt as if she was talking to an old friend. The lady was simply wonderful. Her gestures were kind. She was compassionate and empathetic. She completed each sentence with a striking smile that reflected her pure heart and intentions.

Clair's eyes went toward the shopping bags she carried with her. Out of curiosity, I asked her about them. "How come you have so many bags today?"

She told her that she had bought a pink stuffed bunny for a patient and some other gifts for the rest. She showed the gifts to me with excitement. She even told me that one of the girls was fond of red flowers; thus, she had brought one for her. Clair, working at the hospital, didn't know this about her patients…but the lady did. Her eyes were filled with love when she talked about them.

She asked her the reason behind all that she did for the patients at the hospital, and the lady commented: "Every day that you manage to bring someone else joy, this can never be a wasted day."

"You should be proud of yourself for being such a kind human being," Clair said with love and admiration. The lady patted Clair on the back and said, "Honey, you are a good girl, so I have to tell you my secret, which is: give without expecting anything in return. Be the one who makes someone happy and gives another person a reason to smile. In this day and age, there are a handful of people who will do the same. Be one of them, and bring the change of happiness and love. Commit to creating joy all around you and watch the magic unfold."

Clair still remembers the spark in the lady's eyes when she told her this. She is one of her role models. After that day, whenever Clair came into the hospital, she brought with her the desire and commitment to make the day a little brighter for all those whom she came in contact with.

This simple but powerful change not only transformed her enjoyment of her job, but a magical spark would also follow her home to her family and linger well past her working hours.

Paper Flowers

I was sitting at my desk, working on a new project. My eyes dropped to the precious paper flower I placed carefully in a pen stand. I picked it up, and an innocent face flashed in my mind. It reminded me of my visit to Pender Island. The experience was still fresh in my mind.

Pender Island is a hidden jewel located on the west coast in British Columbia. It is home to about 2,250 permanent residents, as well as a large seasonal population. Pender Island has a sub-Mediterranean climate and features open farmland, rolling forested hills, several lakes, and small mountains, as well as many coves and beaches.

Its breathtaking beauty and warm weather make it easy to become enchanted by this remote place. For the last ten years, my husband and I always look forward to our annual visit to this heaven on earth. It is an amazing place to go to when you really want to just rest.

I have lovingly referred to Pender as a forgotten world. What I mean by this is that in some wonderful way, it feels like stepping back in time.

As I write this, I see children carelessly playing and laughing while chasing a red ball. Two older gentlemen are engaged in a game of chess outside of the town's bakery. The locals smile freely and extend warmth to all of those they come into contact with.

The Saturday market is a phenomenon that both locals and tourists look forward to. There is an abundance of locally grown fruits and vegetables in all the colors of a rainbow. Homemade jams and crafts of all sorts draw you in to take a closer look. It never ceases to amaze me as to how many different talents are out there. There are wooden jewelry boxes made to perfection. Knitted clothes for children and handmade aprons. Ceramic plates and vases of stunning quality. Freshly made bread and pastries fill the air with irresistible aromas, making us hungry despite the substantial breakfast enjoyed earlier. It is truly heavenly.

It is heartwarming to witness the warm exchange from the locals when they greet each other. This is a community where people seem to know and care about one another.

Pender has a number of memorable destinations, such as the Renaissance gallery. Milada and Jan Huk, the owners, are highly educated and charming individuals who possess many treasures in their gallery. Milada, who holds a Ph.D. in art history, makes stunning jewelry from Swarovski crystals.

The gallery has unique antiques from different parts of the world, including limited edition lithographs as well as some originals from the old masters. This was an unexpected but wonderful surprise.

Next on our list of favorites comes the Sea Star winery, which is nestled in the rolling hills of Pender's majestic beauty. The tasting room and welcoming patio make it a great place to relax and enjoy some wonderful local white wine on a warm summer day.

On this magical island, there are hidden surprises every step of the way. Wildlife roams freely thorough old grown forests. Stunning vistas are seen on the many hiking trails available, which range from moderate for beginners to ambitious ones for the seasoned hiker.

LIFE IS NOW

The morning coffees we sipped sitting on the patio of the cottage we rented were nothing short of incredible. It wasn't simply the coffee, but the ambiance and environment of this beautiful place that helped put all of my worries behind me. It is so peaceful that one can only hear the sounds of birds chirping and waves of water from the sea hitting the shore. I have to say that I found it to be a truly meditative experience. The sound of bald eagles communicating with each other was unmistakable. These majestic birds were rare and welcomed sight.

If I had to choose what I love most about our time spent in Pender, it would have to be what I genuinely felt in my heart. Peace.

The warmth and openness of the locals appealed to the most human part of me. A local lady told me a story of when she got pregnant and gave birth at the age of forty-seven. She and her husband had given up their hopes and expectations of ever having a child. However, the gift of life presented itself to them after many years. Life is truly full of surprises.

This miracle child was welcomed by the whole community. Handmade blankets and clothing were lovingly made for this little boy. As the saying goes, it takes a village to raise a child, and he had an entire community ready to love, care, and support him.

On our last visit, we walked into the local art gallery, which was a partial bookstore as well. There was a little girl who was busy drawing with markers. She greeted me with a warm smile, and since I love children, it really made me feel warm on the inside. To my surprise, a couple of minutes later, she walked up to me and handed me a small drawing of a flower. When I thanked her, she just smiled and walked away. This spontaneous gesture of kindness really touched me. As I spent time perusing books, I realized that the little girl was closely watching everyone who entered the store. I noticed that after a while, another lady walked into the store. The little girl also handed her a paper flower, and she was visibly delighted. I didn't understand how this girl was choosing whom to give flowers to, but I noticed that she was studying all the new people who were coming in through the entrance of the store.

    I was happy that this little girl was growing up in a place that was filled with love, enough so that she was comfortable in expressing her love to others as well. The simple act of handing me a paper flower made me understand that a random act of kindness goes a long way in making someone feel happy. Honestly, you never know when someone could use a paper flower from a pure soul. It truly did wonders for me.

LIFE IS NOW

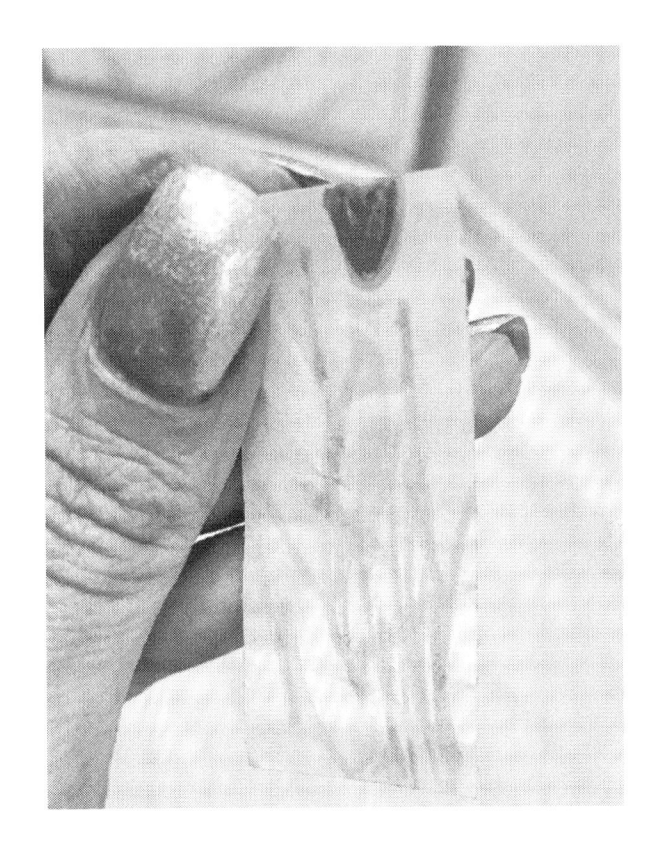

Becoming a Healer—Russell's Story

Dr. Russell Graham is tall and thin with wavy, light brown hair. He is a very fit man who walks his talk.

Russell is a naturopathic physician, a humanitarian, and an animal rights activist. I have known him for more than twenty years, and I am fortunate to be able to call him a friend.

I would lovingly refer to Russell as the doctor who brings nobility to the profession. The way he treats his patients by giving them unconditional love and respect is proof of his heartwarming personality.

Life sometimes takes a turn that may bring out the best in you. You might feel like the transformation is harsh, but later on, you will realize that it contributed as a gift toward making you what you are right now. The same thing happened with him, which unmasked the hero hiding inside Russell. His journey toward becoming a healer was tough, but it was valuable.

When I met Russell, he told me that at the age of nineteen, when most of us are feeling invincible, Russell was forced to deal with a counter-reality. He was diagnosed with testicular cancer. We never talked about it in depth until recently. This experience shaped the rest of his life.

The cancer was surgically removed from one of the testicles. Being malignant in nature, the tumor spread aggressively into his lungs before the chemotherapy sessions were started. The next couple of years were spent fighting the battle for life. Russell's mother was always there by his side. She sought alternative ways of supporting her son through this ordeal.

One thing is sure, and this young man did not have the luxury to take his health for granted, as most of us had when we were young. Instead, Russell was trying different diets and treatments that might help facilitate his recovery. Some turned out to be a success, while others didn't.

It took a couple of years for Russell to regain his strength. He dealt with digestion problems for years to follow. Russell discovered at an early age that health was a blessing that should be regarded with great care.

As he started to heal, he was thrilled to travel and explore the treasures of the orient with his girlfriend. He was happy to be able to start living some of his dreams.

After finishing his teaching degree, Russell revealed that he would prefer to devote his life to the realm of wellness and health. The desire to help those suffering beaconed him. As a result, Russell enrolled himself in a naturopathic school. He was accepted to some of the best schools in Canada, as well as the US, which was both flattering and encouraging. He completed his degree in 1997 and has been in practice since then.

Today, he is sixty. He is healthy and active and looks at least ten years younger than his age. Russell told me that this experience gave him a number of gifts that brought joy to every aspect of his life. He learned that life and health are blessings that we usually forget to be grateful for. When he was young, the biggest challenge for him was to regain confidence that he would have the strength to live his dreams without fearing for his health.

Russell finds his work both satisfying and rewarding. He reconsidered his career choices and found this profession as the best way to help people who were going through similar problems that he had to overcome. Since he suffered from similar circumstances during his illness, he can understand the pain of his patients better, making him a more sympathetic and empathetic doctor. He doesn't want others to go through a worsening health condition just because of an imbalanced diet and lifestyle.

From his journey, I receive a message of hope, a message about never giving up in life, no matter what complications it throws our way. I was reminded that health is wealth and how a person could use his greatest challenge as strength and inspiration to help others. For Russell, what I can say is keep doing what you're doing—you're an inspiration. This world needs more loving and devoted doctors like you.

Parting words...

Dear Past,

Thank you for the lessons.

On a parting note, I want to thank you all for honoring me with your time. I hope that some of the love that went into writing this book will linger with you.

For whatever it is worth, here are some suggestions from someone who loves nothing more than to see people smile.

- Love freely; there is no better way to grow.
- Smile often, even if you have to force it. You might be amazed by the fact that you'll feel instantly better; maybe the next one will be real.
- Forgive easily.
- Taste every sip of your coffee.
- Do not put another bite of food in your mouth before tasting the first one.
- Give hugs generously. Especially to the elderly, a loving touch can be healing.
- Time goes by fast—might as well have some fun along the way.
- You can't afford to take yourself too seriously. It seems to suck the fun out of life.
- Ask yourself if what you are about to say is intelligent, useful, or at least funny.
- If the words in your head are mean-spirited, it's probably a good idea to keep them to yourself. Words can be really hurtful and take a long time to heal.
- Celebrate even small victories. It is much easier to win the game of life this way. This will train your mind to look for ways to appreciate life and celebrate often.

- Make time to read. Read something every day. I love reading something empowering first thing in the morning. It helps me begin my day positively.
- Do things to bring a break to your routine. Be spontaneous. We tend to remember the things we did differently.
- Knowing our own weaknesses can be a great strength.
- Seek the company of positive, supportive people. Stop and notice how you feel around them.
- Keep the inner child alive and well. I still hug every stuffed toy before gifting it to a child.
- If we spend our time angry about the past and fearful of the future, we never have the best of us available to enjoy the present moment.
- Take a few moments here and there to listen to the beautiful song of a bird, notice the new leaves in spring, and gaze at the stars. Fall in love with life, and it will fall in love with you.

If you enjoyed this book, then I invite you to participate in my upcoming one, titled:

Ordinary Extraordinary People Living Ordinary Extraordinary Lives

If you have a story you would like to share about anyone with a different and outstanding life, then please send it to us.

We will make sure that you and the authors are credited for their contributions.

Thank you!

Lucie Marlo

Made in the USA
Middletown, DE
24 July 2020